WE SHOULD GET TOGETHER

WE SHOULD GET TOGETHER

The Secret to Cultivating Better Friendships

Written and illustrated by

KAT VELLOS

Subjects: Non-fiction, Friendship, Interpersonal Relations, Happiness, Communication and Social Skills, Personal Growth, Psychology, Self Help, Self Actualization

Interior and cover design by Kat Vellos
Set in Baskerville, Fira Sans, Bebas, and the illustrator's handwriting

For information about special discounts for bulk purchases, interviews, speaking engagements, or anything else, reach out at weshouldgettogether.com

Hardcover ISBN: 237-0-00075-256-7
Paperback ISBN: 978-1-73437-971-6
Ebook ISBN: 978-1-73437-973-0

To all my friends near and far

Contents

Part 3

Bold new approaches for cultivating friendship, and next steps

INTRODUCTION

French fries are more delicious when you're not eating them alone. It was a beautiful Saturday afternoon in Oakland, my schedule was wide open, and I wanted to share some time with a friend. The only problem was, I didn't have anyone to hang out with. I had recently moved into my own apartment, so didn't have a smattering of roommates around anymore. The few local friends I had were already promised to other commitments they'd set up weeks before—which seemed to be a recurring pattern. To help myself feel less alone, I posted a message on Facebook: "Who wants to go eat french fries and talk about life with me?"

In that moment, my tiny wish felt impossible to fulfill. Nearly everyone who replied to me on Facebook lived in another state. And there was a bigger wish behind my post. I didn't just want to eat snacks and *talk* about life. I was craving a different *kind* of life—one that would give me abundant access to friends who wanted to see me as much as I wanted to see them.

ME
JUNE 13, 2015

• • •

WHO WANTS TO GO EAT FRENCH FRIES AND TALK ABOUT LIFE WITH ME?

👍 40 FRIENDS   26 COMMENTS

 HOW I WISH I WAS IN PROXIMITY!

 I WOULD BUT I'M IN THE CITY!

 ME! I MISS YOU!

 OH KAT! I WOULD LOVE TO. IF ONLY.

 ☹

 BRB, INVENTING TELEPORTATION

 THAT SOUNDS AWESOME!

I'd been living in the Bay Area for a year and a half. I loved my job in San Francisco and my neighborhood on the border of Oakland and Berkeley. But I was lonely. Loneliness was an unfamiliar feeling, and its arrival in my life puzzled me because I wasn't socially isolated. I was surrounded by smart, funny, interesting people who I was constantly meeting at every brunch, meetup, and dinner party I went to. On weekends there were dozens of exciting events and activities to attend. I had a great time at potlucks, meetups, and events but I rarely got to see the people I met there anywhere else. The person-to-person intimacies didn't grow. When I wanted someone just to hang out with, aside from a couple of roommates who were often running around with their own lives, I was usually on my own.

When I moved into my own one-bedroom apartment, I was thrilled beyond words. I'd wanted my own little sanctuary for so long. I thought that having my own place meant that I'd be able to have people over all the time, but it only happened a fraction of the time. Often when I asked my local friends to hang out, they weren't free and wouldn't be for a while. Life seemed to be telling me that I had crossed a new milestone of adulthood:

18th birthday: You get to vote!
21st birthday: You get to drink!
35th birthday: You get to make plans six weeks in
advance any time you want to see a friend!

So in the summer of 2015, I did what I thought any normal person would do. I started a couple meetup groups around topics that matter to me. (I've since been informed that this is not what any normal person would do.) I organized a professional community group for other Black people who practice design (my line of work) and I created an event called *Better than Small Talk* for people who value good conversation. Both meetups were successful, accumulating hundreds of members, and *Bay Area Black Designers* was even profiled in *Forbes*. Running both groups over the next four years required a herculean amount of work, and ironically, they only provided me with a few reliable friends that I got to see away from the meetups. When I wasn't running those groups, I devoted time and energy to deepening connections with my tiny set of local friends. Turning lovely acquaintances into close friends was my passion project.

One day I wrote down the names of all the people I really liked and wanted to be better friends with. One by one, I set out trying to nurture and develop each friendship. I'd contact the person and set up a get-together for tea, a meal, or an activity. We'd share conversation and get to know each other better. Repeat.

It worked with a few people:

• Adrian became a good buddy, but then he started a business. All his time got sucked into doing that, understandably.

• Jabu became a dear friend that I admire and love deeply, but then she moved from the overpriced Bay Area to a gorgeous house for half the price in the southwest United States.

• Marjorie became a semi-regular hangout buddy for about a year. Then we both got into relationships and found ourselves spending more of our free time with our partners. Our texts and hangouts went extinct.

• Once, someone on a listserv that I was in wrote the group saying that she was looking for a roommate. I saw that we lived two blocks apart. I emailed her and said that I didn't want to be her roommate since I already had a place to live, but asked if she wanted to be neighbor friends? She did! We got dinner at a Thai restaurant on the corner, and had a great conversation full of laughs and things in common. But then the new friendship spark fizzled out. We texted a couple times after that but we never managed to hang out again.

• Feeling like I'd struck gold, I got lucky when a few friends moved to the Bay Area from other cities where I'd previously lived. I tried especially hard to nurture these pre-existing friendships. But most of these friends moved away less than two years later. Going-away parties became a regular occurrence, and with each one, more air was let out of my balloon.

I made attempts with many more people, with similarly frustrating results. Making friends as an adult, I'd discovered, is *work*. It's not like being a kid on the playground where having the same color sneakers or a fondness for swings is enough to call someone a friend. It's not like being in high school where simply sitting around the same people every day in class is enough common ground to knit you together during the afternoons and weekends too. And it's not like college where being roommates or classmates is enough to cement your common bond and then, poof, you're best friends for life.

Nope. Building friendships and community as an adult—especially in a new city—is hard work. It's such hard work that some folks have told me they've given up trying, and they're not

the only ones. The average American hasn't made one new friend in the last five years.[1] But the price we pay for giving up is just too high. As we age, research shows that we get more isolated from the people around us.[2] We feel more lonely, and have a harder time making close friends. Nearly half of Americans say they feel alone or left out most of the time. One in four Americans don't feel like there's anyone who really understands them.[3] The loneliness and isolation epidemic flies under the radar, damaging our health and wellbeing every step of the way. Loneliness and isolation wreak havoc on our internal systems: shortening our lifespan and increasing our chances of a multitude of health problems.[4] According to former Surgeon General Vivek H. Murthy, loneliness puts as much stress on our body as smoking fifteen cigarettes a day.[5]

I believe that the experience of community and human connection are as important to our health and well-being as having access to clean air, water, and food. We can live in a vacuum of isolation or a web of connection; either situation will significantly impact how we live our lives and how much happiness, health, and fulfillment we experience along the way.

While starting over in a new city is exciting, it frequently means struggling to satisfy the basic human need for belonging and connection. Meeting new people and forming strong positive connections takes constant effort, and results aren't guaranteed. Cultivating friendship is like nurturing a garden. You clear a patch of land, prepare the beds, and assess which seeds and plants are the best fit for the location and season. You make sure that you'll have the right amount of water, soil, and light. You plant your favorite seeds. And then you invest time and energy into caring for these newly growing things. As they send out shoots and start growing, you hope like hell that you don't forget to water them or get struck with a heat spell—either of which could kick the life out of these baby sprouts and leave you back where you started with bare earth and a handful of tiny wishes. *We Should Get Together* is your guide to becoming a green thumb at cultivating friendships that last.

Over the course of writing this book, I spent a lot of time talking to people about how they experience friendship and community as adults. In my day-to-day life, I'm a professional user experience designer. In simple terms, that means that I investigate the challenges people face when trying to accomplish a certain task, and then I design solutions that solve those problems. Based on my experiences and those of the people I spoke to, I realized that *adult friendship has a user experience problem*. Despite having more ways to meet and keep in contact with friends near and far, many people have fewer close friends and less fulfilling experiences of friendship than ever before. Intrigued, I threw myself into understanding this conundrum. I used a range of methods to help me understand how the problem manifested itself in people's lives, and what allowed some people to transcend it.

I used four types of qualitative research to investigate this problem: generative (defining the problem), descriptive (describing the problem), causal (figuring out what causes the problem) and evaluative (identifying what solutions exist and how successful they are). To answer these questions, I conducted one-on-one interviews, group discussions, telephone interviews, and email interviews. I spoke to hundreds of people about this topic over the last five years, and surveyed sixty-five of them in depth. I bolstered my qualitative research efforts with an extensive litera-ture review of quantitative studies, as well as books and articles. I pored over existing research about friendship, happiness, loneli-ness, health, technology, and the effect of cities and modern life on interpersonal relationships. In doing so, I was able to learn about patterns of human connection and disconnection for adults living in cities, logged from as far back as 1938 to as recently as 2019.

I've attempted to summarize academic findings while also retaining the heart, humanity, and emotion that are at the core of this topic. To create a manageable scope, I focused on how people who live in larger cities experience adult friendship, as opposed to those in the suburbs or rural areas. Many people were kind, brave, and extremely candid in sharing their personal stories with me during the events and interviews that led to the creation of

this book. To protect their privacy, their names have been changed, except for when they gave permission to use their real names.

Throughout the book, you will find firsthand accounts from some of the people I spoke to, as well as practical strategies that have worked well for me and other people living in similar conditions. I talked to people across a wide variety of ages, genders, ethnicities, and occupations. I've listened to their stories of connection and disconnection, their feelings of isolation and hopefulness, their struggles with achieving the kind of closeness that would let them feel like they know others deeply and are deeply known in return. I've heard people recount feelings of helplessness while watching burgeoning friendships stall out, break down, or never fully attain their potential. I've heard others tearfully describe the heart-breaking collapse of long-term friendships. And I've heard people describe the feeling of triumph that comes when they are feeling truly connected with their deepest friends—or when they're feeling something deeply friend-ship-like with a total stranger.

In addition to being a user experience designer, I'm also a facil-itator. Over the last eighteen years I've led workshops, gatherings, events, and facilitated sessions designed to help people cultivate their creativity and connect authentically. I often call upon my facilitation skills whenever I encounter problems in the realm of human interaction.

For example, it was really hard for me to form durable friendships during my first few years in the Bay Area; I was also frustrated by the neverending surface-level chit-chat at every social gathering I went to. So I created an experimental gathering called *Better than Small Talk*. I don't ascribe to the belief that people need weeks or months of time to arbitrarily pass before they can move from superficial conversation to topics that are deeper, more thoughtful, or more personal. It's absolutely possible to cut through the chit-chat and connect authentically more quickly. I know it's possible because I've seen it happen over and over again.

I first learned this in 2006, when I trained as a facilitator with an organization called Partners for Youth Empowerment (formerly The Power of Hope). Over the next several years I led hundreds of hours of workshops and programs with them. I've facilitated community-building workshops for youth and adults everywhere from middle school classrooms to conferences and weeklong overnight camps. I've seen the power of creating safe environments where people can express themselves and be fully seen and accepted for who they really are. It can dramatically transform the way people relate to each other.

One of my favorite activities from my time working for Power of Hope was called Milling. You take a room full of people and instruct them to move around the room—sometimes in creative ways like pretending to walk through waist-deep molasses or imagining that they're tiptoeing through the house to sneak out at midnight. Periodically we'd interrupt and pair people off to answer questions. We'd ask questions that ignite the imagination and invite people to share more about themselves, like:

- What's something you gave up to be here tonight, and something you're looking forward to?
- What's something you love about where you live and something you'd change?
- If you had a microphone and the whole world was listening, what would you say?

I love seeing how much people open up when asked simple questions and are earnestly listened to. Inevitably, their walls start to come down and they begin to feel connected to each other. *Better than Small Talk* was designed as an immersive experience around the same premise as Milling. I held it in Oakland, Berkeley, Seattle, and L.A., and experimented with different formats each time. Sometimes the gathering was an intimate dinner for seven. Sometimes people moved organically through a room filled with conversation-starter questions pinned to clotheslines. Other times I led a room full of people through guided meditation

and prompted conversation in pairs or small groups. Usually all the participants were strangers.

Participants often said that the conversations they had during *Better than Small Talk* were deeper and felt more grounded than their conversations with people in their daily lives. Just a couple hours before the event, they were literally strangers, but afterwards many of them said—sometimes with tears in their eyes—that they felt like close friends. Sometimes people would leave the gathering hugging each other, making plans to extend the evening, or trading phone numbers with their newfound buddies. The goal of *Better than Small Talk* wasn't to make sure everyone left with a best friend—it was simply to give people access to an alternate reality that provided them with inspiring tools and a shared context upon which connection can be easily built. This is one of the many reasons why I believe that when given the right space and practical tools, friendship and community can develop quickly and abundantly.

I believe that deep conversations, in which we disclose the

more sensitive emotions, thoughts, and feelings that we'd otherwise hold inside, are superior in every way to superficial conversation. Deep conversations are also correlated with greater happiness than surface-level conversation, as Mattias Mehl, a psychologist at the University of Arizona, has reported in *The New York Times* and *Psychology Today*.[6] The problem is, our lives are too often starved for this type of vulnerable, bonding interaction. I'm not the only one who's noticed this social deficit and tried to help fix it. In my research during this book, I learned about a multitude of other groups, organizations, and games that exist to help people access deep, meaningful conversation with the people around them. For example: The Ungame was invented in 1972, Conversation Cafe has been worldwide for over a decade, Free Intelligent Conversation is held in public spaces nationwide, Big Talk cards are available all over the world, Chatty Cafe is held in the U.K., End Small Talk (which I did one cross-continent collaboration event with) is held in Dubai, Tea with Strangers is held nationwide. In late 2019 even famous behavioral economist Dan Ariely started selling a deck of No Small Talk cards on his lab's website. Additionally, there are hundreds if not thousands of meetups that invite people to make new friends via the practice of authentic conversation.

I started my friendship experiments and research in earnest in the San Francisco Bay Area because I felt that there was something unusually challenging about this place and the people who are drawn to it. It is the only place I've ever lived where I've had a hard time forming strong, reliable friendships. While I do think that it's especially hard here—and I've uncovered research that proves it, which we'll explore later—I'd found that this is a challenge for people all over the United States and even beyond its borders. Yet we rarely talk about this problem. This quiet desperation doesn't even have a name, but a great many of us have felt it before. I call it *platonic longing*. This book is for everyone who has ever known this quiet ache:

• If you never want to hear the questions "What do you do?" and "Where are you originally from?" ever again because when you're surrounded by real friends, no one needs to ask that.

• If you've ever had to care for your horrible cold, surgery recovery, or chronic pain all by yourself because there wasn't a single friend or neighbor who would come through your door to check on you.

• If you've ever had a stroke of good fortune and wanted someone to celebrate it with, but instead sat with your joyous moment alone because no one was free to hang out.

• If you've spent more time watching Netflix over the last six months than you've spent talking to people who know the land-scape of your inner world.

• If you've ever gone on a dating app wondering, "Would this work if I said 'I'm just looking for friends?'" Or if you've tried the friend-making apps too and found that the great friendships they promised still haven't materialized.

• If you spend more time holding hands with your phone than holding hands with a friend.

Don't worry—this book isn't only about the struggles. It's also about the strategies and tools that will help you cultivate robust friendships. *We Should Get Together* is for anyone who wants to have dedicated, life-enriching friends, and who wants to be that kind of friend, too.

• For anyone who wants to know others deeply and be known deeply in return.

• For anyone who is brave enough to strike up a new kind of conversation, reaching past small talk towards topics that make your heart and brain vibrate with meaningful thoughts and deep feelings.

• For anyone who is improving their cooking and baking skills, and wishing for more great people in their life to break delicious bread with.

• For anyone cultivating their friendship garden: watering the seeds, pulling the weeds, and reaching for the sweet fruit of human connection.

Put simply, this book is for anyone who wants to create more meaningful friendships in their life. In the following pages, I'll be your guide to making that a reality. I'll also be right there beside you, going through a lot of the same friendship struggles. We'll dig into why friendship during adulthood is so often a challenge, as well as strategies that you can start using right away to make things better. I can't promise that what's worked well for others will definitely work for you; everyone's situation is different. I only offer these suggestions humbly in an attempt to provide insights that might be useful to you in your own life. I hope the stories and advice on these pages help you feel less alone and inspire you to find ways to bring more enriching experiences of friendship into your life.

As part of my research for this book I polled 65 American adults between the ages of 20 and 70 in depth about their experiences of friendship and community.

an acquaintance is:

Someone I know basic details about

Someone I've met but have no deep emotional connection to

Someone that I know in passing. I may say hi but will not go out of my way to meet up.

Someone I can just have small talk with

Someone I've met in person a few times but who I wouldn't contact to hang out

A limited, superficial relationship, like a friend of a friend

a close friend is:

Someone whose wellbeing I care deeply about and who I feel confident I can depend on

Someone I make time to see regularly one on one

Someone who accepts me completely for who I am

If I'm in trouble or going through a rough patch, they are there with me till the end

Someone I can confide in, am comfortable being vulnerable with, and whose advice I seek

Someone I would hop on a plane to help at a moment's notice and vice versa

One question asked people how they'd define an acquaintance, a friend, and a close friend. These answers are great examples of the total sample and are good to keep in mind as you go through the rest of the book.

a friend is:

Someone I've formed a connection with, and that I'd be glad if they called/texted/invited me

Someone I don't see very often but genuinely enjoy when I do. If I throw a party, they're on the list.

Someone I feel safe and happy with, and that I wanna hang out more with

Someone I see relatively often and tell the details of my life to, however, they are not someone I rely on when I am in trouble

Someone I know well. We know each other's life circumstances and how we got to be who we are.

Someone I don't have to try hard to have a conversation with

Someone I would discuss intimate details of my life with

Someone I would go out of my way for, or ask a favor of, or hang out and really talk deeply with

Someone who knows my secrets, fears, and who tells me what I need to hear even if I don't like it

Someone I never feel like I need to entertain

Someone I can tell my problems to without feeling ashamed

Someone who is integrated into my life

HOW FRIENDSHIP GOT SO COMPLICATED

Friendship. It's supposed to be so simple. You live your life, you make some friends. Want a friend? Make a friend. Easy. They come and go. No big deal. Right? Well, not always. For many of us, making friends was pretty easy when we were young. We're figuring out that it doesn't necessarily stay that way. Forming and maintaining friendships gets harder as we get older and move from city to city, job to job, and life stage to ever-more-complicated life stage. Friendship—as a concept and as an experience—changes, just like everything else.

For one thing, friendship means different things to different people. In the delightful and sometimes perilous world of dating, "the friend zone" is where you put someone when they have absolutely no chance at getting into your heart or bedroom. The friend zone is the dark corner where rejected crushes go to die. When people decide to split up and they say, "Let's just be friends," what they really mean is, "Let's just be strangers."

What does the word "friend" even mean to us anymore? Social media has made it synonymous with everything from the acquaintances you used to work with at your part-time job ten years ago to the lifelong BFFs who would give you their kidney. On social media, a "friend" might be the cutie you met at the Halloween party, the spybots masquerading as friends of your friends, or the coworkers you sit in meetings with but probably don't invite to hang out at your house after work. We spend more time building our lists of followers and contacts than we spend building real, true friendships.

At the opposite end of the spectrum, the word "friend" is wholly inadequate to describe the deep, loyal, trusted friendships that actually become our chosen family. In adulthood, finding these new family members and integrating them into our lives is getting harder. It's important that we're still able to do so because when we really need help—emotionally, physically, profession-ally, or spiritually—trusted friends are often the ones we call on. When songwriter Bill Withers felt nostalgic after moving to Los Angeles and found himself missing the strong connections and community spirit of his tiny hometown in West Virginia, he didn't write a song called "I've Been Really Busy" or "Maybe We Can Catch Up Next Week." No, Withers wrote the hit song "Lean On Me."[1] Do you know who you can lean on?

You may have heard by now, perhaps a disappointing number of times already, that loneliness and social isolation are on the rise. They're also correlated with having high blood pressure, cardio-vascular disease, poor cognitive functions, depression, personality disorders, dementia, and suicide.[2] A 2018 study by Cigna on lone-liness found that:

- 46 percent of Americans report feeling lonely some or all of the time
- One in four Americans feel like there's no one they can talk to, or like there's no one who understands them
- One in five Americans report that they rarely or never feel close to people[3]

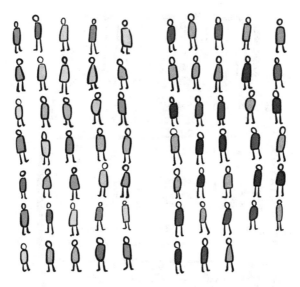

ALMOST HALF OF AMERICANS REPORT
FEELING LONELY SOME OR ALL OF THE TIME

These findings correlate with those of former Surgeon General Vivek Murthy who, after speaking to communities nationwide, reported, "I found that there were a growing number of people who were saying that they felt profoundly alone."[4] It's been over thirty-five years since *The New York Times* Health Editor Jane E. Brody first reported in 1983 that loneliness was a national epidemic in the US, pointing to "our highly technological society" (before the internet, mind you) as one of the contributing factors.[5]

Meaningful friendships aren't just fun. They've also been shown to improve your health, increase your capacity to endure pain,[6] and they can literally help you live longer.[7] To help people live full, healthy, long lives, doctors might need to start handing out

prescriptions for friend time. I'm not kidding. The UK's Minister of Loneliness already recommends that Britain's doctors utilize more social prescribing, which is the act of referring patients to non-medical wellbeing interventions such as art classes, gardening clubs, and cooking classes.[8] In some cases, social prescribing works just as well as pharmaceuticals when it comes to alleviating patients' pain and suffering.[9] Just watch. Prescriptions for quality time with friends is coming next.

I would be remiss if I failed to acknowledge how the world we live in plays a factor in this problem. I'm talking about the actual physical setting that the majority of us choose to call home:

cities. Around 80 percent of Americans (263 million people)[10] and 55 percent of all earth dwellers (4 billion people) choose to live in cities. The population of large urban cities is growing faster than in any other type of place that people live on the planet.[11] The problem is that most cities were not designed to facilitate the friendship and happiness of their residents. In many cases, the physical layout, zoning laws, modes of transportation, and rules governing public spaces are the absolute opposite of what people need in order to experience the health, happiness, autonomy, and interactions that would benefit them the most.[12] As a result, while city life can be exciting and energizing, it can also be exhausting and lonesome.

The hustle and bustle that throws us into each other's paths all day long are also poor sources of quality connections. One notable record of this phenomenon comes from 1938 when the father of modern day sociology, Louis Wirth, attempted to create a sociological definition of the city. Cities overtook rural areas as the primary address for Americans around 1920 but no one had yet attempted to fully document what the impact of this change meant for people's lives. Wirth's report came back peppered with words and phrases like *impersonal, ...anonymity, ...superficiality,... highly fractionalized, ... social disorganization in technological society,... The bonds of kinship, of neighborliness, are likely to be absent,* ... And last but not least: *Frequent close physical contact coupled with great social distance accentuates the reserve of unattached individuals toward one another and, unless compensated for by other opportunities for response, give rise to loneliness.*[13] Wirth's report is easy to find online, and reading it is incredibly cathartic. The way we relate to each other in big

American cities hasn't changed a lot in eighty-one years. So if you've been feeling frustrated or lonely or like it's hard to connect with people in your city, take some solace in the fact that you aren't alone. Big city life has been delivering the paradoxical experience of feeling crowded-yet-alienated for a very long time.

As long as we make cities our number one choice for where to live, we will likely face challenges achieving optimal friendship and community within them. But that doesn't mean we should give up. We can't easily change the structure of the world around us, so let's focus on what we can control: ourselves and what we do with each other while we're here. The only thing that can save us from this isolating conundrum is each other.

When you think about your own friendship landscape, what does it look like? How many durable friendships do you have?

Where are your closest friends located? Who can you have real conversations with or turn to in a crisis? If you want a new best friend, do you know how to make one? If your life is filled with interesting acquaintances, do you know how to convert them into close friends? What do you do when you discover that you're surrounded by people who don't really know who you are?

In my research for this book, I pored over fascinating studies about the factors that contribute to—or inhibit—the formation of friendship. A number of these studies were done on the population of people most readily available to university-funded researchers: college students. This makes their findings only partially usable for an audience of working adults, since numerous factors make it harder for adults to make new friends and to stay close to old ones. Turning new acquaintances into solid friends can be especially tough. When I tried to figure out what made that transformation so hard for me, I realized what was getting in the way: the Big Buts. We all have a few that pop up frequently or impact us the most. Which ones are yours? Go on, check 'em off:

"I'd love to have better friendships...but:

Time

☐ I'd rather use my free time on personal development pursuits.

☐ I'd rather use my free time to exercise and get in shape.

☐ I'd rather use my free time to develop myself professionally and build my career.

☐ I'd rather use my free time to just relax alone.

☐ I have a side hustle or passion project that takes a lot of time.

☐ I keep my schedule so packed, there's no time for friends.

Work & Money

☐ I work a lot, probably too much, but I don't feel like I can change this.

☐ I have long commutes that eat into my free time.

☐ I'm more focused on reaching for success in my career.

☐ I have too many financial demands. I don't have the disposable income to spend on frivolous fun.

☐ I finally make enough money to have disposable

income and I want to spend it on things like travel that don't usually result in friendship.

☐ I make a lot less, or a lot more, than my friends and it creates a strain in our relationships.

Emotional Availability

☐ I need time alone to recharge.

☐ I've been through some challenges in life so I have more walls to break through before I can open up and be vulnerable with new people that I meet.

☐ I don't value friendship as much at this stage of my life.

☐ I don't want to go out as much as I did before. It's too tiring.

☐ I realized that I'm an introvert. Instead of burning myself out socializing, I'm making up for years of lost alone time.

☐ I hardly have enough time to keep up with my friends who live in other cities, so how can I also be there for friends locally?

☐ I'm too harsh on myself when I think about how I've performed in past social interactions, which makes me feel more anxious about hanging out with people in the future.

☐ I'm more guarded, less trusting, and more skeptical about people's intentions. When someone asks to hang out more than twice a month, I start to worry that they're some kind of stalker.

☐ I don't trust strangers. I'm unnerved when someone I don't know speaks to me.

☐ I don't feel comfortable in uncurated interactions where unexpected things might happen.

☐ I'm flaky and constantly ghosting (a.k.a. disappearing, not following up) with potential friends, even after sharing positive experiences together. Or, other people are constantly ghosting on me—it's hard to tell who's just busy vs who doesn't like me.

Location

☐ Everybody else moves too much.

☐ I move too much.

☐ I moved to a place where nobody knows me.

☐ I moved here from really far away and communicating with people is really different here. It's like I'm on another planet.

☐ I live too far away from my friends in this city, so we rarely cross paths spontaneously, and trying to schedule time together is harder than getting a doctor's appointment.

MARY GOT A LITTLE LAMB ... BECAUSE
ALL HER FRIENDS KEPT MOVING AWAY.

☐ I don't know my neighbors. Even though we see each other all the time, I don't consider them friends.

Love & Family

☐ I spend most of my time dating because I'm looking for a romantic partner.

☐ I choose to spend most of my free time with my partner.

☐ I'm busy caring for one or more babies.

☐ I'm busy caring for and raising my child/children.

☐ I'm busy caring for aging parents.

☐ I've become socially isolated via marriage or divorce.

☐ Close family members or friends have passed away and that trauma has impacted my ability to partake in other types of relationships like friendship and socializing.

The Internet

☐ I treat social media as the default place to catch up with friends, instead of in real life.

☐ It's hard to get someone new to meet up face to face, so we just interact online.

☐ I don't have time for a *new* friend because I already have 2,587 friends that I need to scroll past on Facebook, Twitter, Instagram, etc.

Other

_____

_____

What is up with us? Are we really doomed by this ever-growing list of excuses? We have so many Buts. And a lot of possibilities, too— that's what I'm interested in.

Some people say Americans are more lonely now than they were in the past due to rising mobility, divorce, and distrust. They say that our forebears were less lonely because they had smaller social circles to manage, and people were more deeply connected to the people they knew. Others say that our forebears were lonelier in the past because of geographical, technological, and social limitations. They say that we're less lonely now because we have more ways of keeping in touch, more social acceptance for different kinds of people, and more convenient transportation options to reach everyone.

This back and forth is like arguing about air pollution in the past compared to now. Some say the air is horrible now because of cars and industry, and some say that the air was worse in the past because of coal-burning locomotives and factories. In either case, what's a good amount of pollution to have in the air? None. I'm not here to argue about when times were better or worse. The fact is, loneliness is the emotional pollution of our time, and it's all around us.

Just like we can't talk about how to address climate change without talking about the things that contribute to it, we can't talk about how to fix the friendship problem without acknowledging and examining its contributing factors. We need to know what we're up against. That said, I didn't want to write a thirty-five-volume encyclopedia, and I'm sure you don't want to read a book that's a bazillion pages long. You won't find an in-depth exploration here of every single challenge on that list of Big Buts above. We will be exploring the ones that I've found to be most common: hypermobility, busyness, relationships/family, and the shrinking capacity for intimacy in the digital era.

Also, we're primarily focusing on friendships that can be explored in person. While virtual friendships can also be meaningful and alleviate the pain of isolation, the value of in-person friendships cannot be denied. The ideas, research, and suggestions in the following chapters can help you to increase the number of friends you have, or deepen and fortify existing friendships. Each section has several exercises and reflection questions, so I encourage you to keep a journal handy. Explore, enjoy, and have fun.

HYDROPONIC FRIENDSHIP

In an ideal world, everyday life would bubble over with the perfect conditions for friendship. We would all have abundant quantities of free time to spend with friends, even daily if we wanted to. We'd eat meals together, go on walks, play sports and games, take classes, attend concerts, museums, and movies, volunteer together, and still have time left over for long heart-to-heart talks and peaceful relaxed silences. We'd be able to step out our front door and walk to a dozen friends' houses in under ten minutes. Whenever any of us was in need of physical or emotional support, we would not hesitate to ask, and we'd have plenty of people available to comfort and assist us. It would basically look like life on all those movies and TV shows about friends.

But in reality, it's not that easy. For starters, making and maintaining friendships takes time and most of us feel like we don't have enough of that precious resource. In a study called "How Many Hours Does It Take to Make a Friend," Dr. Jeffrey Hall, a professor at the University of Kansas, found that it takes ninety to 200 hours to turn a stranger or acquaintance into a close friend.[1] This was under typical undergrad circumstances in which the study participants had abundant free time, similar schedules, and lived in close proximity to each other. A key factor in the students' success forming new friends was having a large quantity of interactions. When I look back at my life, that seems to be true. Some of the people I was friends with in my teens and twenties were pretty random, but life circumstances (and sometimes jobs) had us around each other so much that our friendship just happened.

I respect the work of Dr. Hall and his colleagues, but after reading this study I was left feeling a mix of skepticism and optimism. I was skeptical when I thought about all the people who will feel hopeless when they hear that number—200 hours to make a friend?!—because they don't have a lot of free time, they're lonely right now, and they're getting their friend-time in two-hour blocks, often weeks or months apart. At the same time, I felt buoyed by my own observation that it's possible to establish a friendship faster than that. I agree that the quantity of time spent together matters—it matters a lot. But I don't believe it's the only way. As a result of my own successful experiments bringing meaningful connection into the lives of busy adults who need and want friends, I firmly believe that a robust immersion in quality connection marked by vulnerability, self-disclosure, and empathetic listening, experienced in a concentrated form, can fast-track a friendship into existence in a shorter amount of time.

I call this *hydroponic friendship*. In the absence of abundant soil (aka abundant time), nutrients (aka deeply-enriching, immersive experiences of connection) can be supplied to the plant (aka people) in such a way that growth (aka friendship) can fully blossom and thrive. In 1929, William Frederick Gericke, the father of modern-day hydroponics, faced harsh skepticism from his professional peers when he suggested that a garden can be grown in water instead of soil.[2] Today we accept this as unremarkable fact. The time is ripe for an era of hydroponic friendship. It's not only possible, but our modern life has made it necessary. The old pace of life that supported the slow and natural development of effortless friendship is harder and harder to come by. Strategic interventions and passionate intentions will be required.

Realizing friendship fulfillment as working adults requires us to intentionally shift our expectations and our behavior in order to cope with the challenges we face. We don't expect other things—like a romantic connection—to magically appear in our lives with no effort of our own, so we can't expect that to happen for friendship either. These connections require dedicated attention and a willingness to apply ourselves. Just like it's possible to develop a romantic relationship when partners agree to make it a priority, we can also nurture nascent and anemic friendships to become more satisfying and successful. Like baking a cake, we can add the right ingredients in the right amounts and make something delicious.

I believe that the same passion and ingenuity that allows us to conceive of and create new art, medical advancements, and technologies can also be employed to help us dream up, create, and optimize the most important thing that we as humans will ever do: connect with each other in life-enriching, life-expanding ways that fill our days with meaning and make this life worth living.

On the following pages, you'll encounter the stories of people dealing with difficulty in the world of friendship, as well as stories from people who have figured out how to overcome our most frequent obstacles. What you find on these pages will comfort and inspire you, and give you the tools to cultivate a more beautiful friendship garden of your own.

COMPATIBILITY

PROXIMITY

FREQUENCY

COMMITMENT

SEEDS OF CONNECTION

I spent a lot of time over the last several years studying, experimenting with, and interviewing people about their experiences of friendship. Many times I heard stories about friendships falling apart or it feeling too hard to get them started in the first place. Yet there were a lot of stories about successful friendships too—ones where each person felt fulfilled, happy, and grateful for the durability of their friendships. Patterns began to emerge, revealing why some friendships falter and others thrive. I have identified a number of ingredients that are core to the creation and continuation of quality friendships. I call them the Seeds of Connection: proximity, frequency, compatibility and commitment.

The more you cultivate these critical components in burgeoning or existing friendships, the greater your likelihood of success. When they're lacking due to circumstance or not being actively nurtured, the greater your likelihood of failure. All of the seeds are important, but you may find that some matter more to you than others.

As we'll explore, each of them can come in more than one form. If you're trying to keep old friendships alive with people who live hundreds of miles away, proximity will obviously matter the least, though you might want to think about bumping frequency or commitment to the top of the list. If you're trying to make friends in the new city you just moved to, proximity will matter a lot and you should think about making it your priority. Let's explore each of these characteristics more in depth.

Proximity

Proximity refers to the geographical and physical closeness that makes it easy to cross paths and share space in the tangible world. For our purposes, proximity means that you and your friends can meet up face to face. In social psychology, the proximity principle explains why people who are physically close to each other will have a higher chance of forming a meaningful connection.[1]

If you think living nearby doesn't matter, consider this: As reported in the book *Who's Your City*, researchers at the University of London found that if a person moves away from a place where they have daily face-to-face interactions with friends and family, they will have to earn an extra $133,000 to make up for the unhappiness and social disconnection that their relocation causes.[2]

Another important aspect of proximity is whether you and your potential friends are both new in town or long-term locals. For simplicity, let's use the terms newcomers and long-termers. Often, long-termers are not open to newcomers, preferring to spend their time and energy with other long-termers who they know will be sticking around. Forming and maintaining friendships is a big investment of time and energy. If a newcomer is going to skip town in six months and leave the long-termers behind with no one to hang out with, the long-termers may think that building a friendship with them is a waste of time and effort. On the flip side, newcomers tend to make easy connections with other newcomers because of the shared experience of being in a new environment and interested in discovering their new surroundings.

Proximity has another advantage. It contributes to overall feelings of belonging. When I was in my early twenties, I lived in a small town in northeast Florida where I could reach eight different friends by walking less than ten minutes from my front door. Even if I wasn't seeing each person every day, I felt "at home" just passing by their houses and knowing that they were inside. I firmly believe that home isn't an address—it's wherever you feel like you belong. Home is anywhere people notice, and care, when they don't see you around. Having friends in close proximity transforms a generic neighborhood into an extended home.

Another important thing to remember about proximity: friendship is more than a matter of convenience. Yes, it's true, proximity makes it much easier to create or maintain a friendship. It's easy to reach out and touch that which is within arm's reach. But if your friendships are going to be real, then your connection to them should continue to exist even if they move across town, or across the planet. Enduring friendship goes beyond zip codes.

The depth of your existing connection also affects how much proximity matters. If I only get to see my lifelong best friend once every couple years, it's not the same thing as seeing an acquaintance or casual friend at the same rate. The depth of a longstanding friendship can make it possible to withstand long bouts of geographical distance, especially if we keep in touch frequently in other ways.

Proximity is a big deal, but it can't solve all your friendship problems. If it could, then everyone's next door neighbors would be their best friends. In reality, 30 percent of people in the US have never even interacted with their neighbors once.[3] Don't be a part of that statistic. Friend locally. Do the proximity assessment below to figure out where and with whom you want to cultivate better friendship. Then follow up with the Try It suggestions.

Proximity Assessment

Get your journal and create the following lists:
• Friends who live less than 15 minutes away
  Specify by: walking, biking, or driving

• Friends who live 20-60 minutes away
  Specify by: walking, biking, or driving

• Friends who live three or more hours away
  Specify by: car, bus, train, or airplane

Questions for reflection
Where do most of your close friends live in proximity relative to you?

Which list are you most and least satisfied by?

Does seeing the distance between you and your friends make you want to deepen any relationships with the people who are nearby?

Describe an ideal weekend in your life if you could walk to ten friends in under ten minutes?

Be More Neighborly

A friendly neighborhood doesn't just magically happen. It's created through the daily actions of each person who lives there, interacting with every other person. There are simple things you can do to create a more friendly neighborhood, and to make friends with the people in your neighborhood. Where to start:

• Look people in the eye when you pass on the sidewalk. Smile at them and say hello.

• Introduce yourself to new people who move into the area; this can be in person or via a nice note dropped in their mailbox.

• Sit outside and chat with people when they pass.

• If your neighbor has a nice garden, talk to them about it.

• Hold a quarterly neighbor party where you invite neighbors to come over and get to know one another. If once per season feels like too much, then aim for a couple times a year. If your place feels too small, hold it outside on the stoop, driveway, sidewalk, or hallway.

Organize a Neighborhood Social

Pick a local coffee shop that has room for several people to sit together comfortably and chat at a conversational volume. Drop off invitations at your neighbors' doors inviting them to a neighborhood social at that location for two hours on a Saturday afternoon. You don't even have to write your name on the invitations if you want it to feel mysterious and a little magical, but signing the invite is a good way to build community. It lets people know that you're open to being reached out to as well. You might find yourself on the receiving end of other invitations to dinners, game nights, movie nights, and extra baked goods. Who wouldn't like a little more of that? For inspiration, check out teawithstrangers.com, which has tips for putting together successful gatherings like this.

Throw a Random Awesome People Party

In early 2019, I led a workshop about cultivating better friendships. At the start of the session, all the participants were strangers. By the end of the workshop, one participant liked everyone else so much, she invited us all to come eat guacamole and chips and drink wine on her back deck.

She realized that a lot of the people she walks past every day—people she commutes with, sees at the grocery store, passes by on her street—might actually be awesome people that she could connect with. There didn't need to be a sensible story about how she came to know each person—we were just, as she put it, "random awesome people." Look around your life at your closest and most-frequently travelled paths. Are random awesome people right there waiting for a chance to meet you?

Frequency

Frequency is the combination of timing and repetition that allows you to foster fondness and familiarity. With a new friend, frequency plays a huge role in how deep and fast a friendship can grow. It has the power to catalyze intimacy, but it takes dedication. The spark of a new friendship fizzles with every passing day apart. If it takes several weeks and several dozen text messages to get a slot in someone's calendar, your momentum could evaporate. If you had brunch in March and don't hang out again until Labor Day, it might be too late for a real friendship to take root.

As awesome as your new potential friend might be, without adequate frequency, you aren't going to become BFFs. Of course, when something is a big enough priority to someone, they will make room in their calendar and their life to include a new person. See: every romantic relationship ever. The same thing can happen for platonic connections if the potential friends want it to. Returning to Dr. Hall's research, he found that you could become "good friends" if you spend 120-160 hours together over three weeks, and "best friends" if you spend 200 hours together over six weeks. On the flip side, he found that if more than four months pass after your initial meeting, then a real friendship is unlikely to ever fully form.[1] Knowing that college students were the test subjects, how would you adapt those time frames to the constraints of your life as a working adult?

Angelica, an effervescent video producer in San Francisco, had some of the highest scores for satisfaction on my friendship survey. Her trick is to use frequency to her advantage and capitalize on the momentum inherent in brand-new acquaintances and newer

ADULT FRIENDSHIP GYM

SPRINT TRAINING
"Let's catch up soon!"

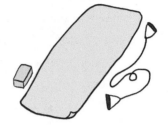

CALENDAR CALISTHENICS
"When's good for you?"

"WAIT" LIFTING
"let me get back to you"

ENDURANCE DRILLS
"What about next month?"

friendships. She relies on people's tendency to be drawn to novelty as a way to increase the depth of her new friendships quickly. "Whenever I meet like-minded people and we feel an instant connection, there's a sense of urgency in that. So we pull out our calendars and make plans for sometime within the next week," she told me. "With my long-term friends there's no sense of urgency, and a lot of them don't reach out to me because they perceive me as someone who's really busy. With a new acquaintance, I can just say 'talk to you tomorrow.'" From there, she quickly invites her new friends into the ongoing hobbies that are already a big part of her life: tennis, playing music, and making videos.[2]

Frequency also matters for maintaining existing friends. Like Angelica and her long-term friends, do you let your frequency lapse because there's no sense of urgency or novelty to excite you? Do you have any existing friendships that are fading away due to a frequency deficit? If you could have more frequency with existing friends, what would it look like?

• Commuting to or from work together
• Swinging by each other's houses after work to
  talk about your day
•Eating an early breakfast or lunch together weekly
• Exercising together a few times a week
• Talking on the phone once or twice a week
• Booking time together around play dates for your kids

Strong friendships often rely on routine to weave the fabric of your lives together. This becomes even more important as we age. Researchers at Michigan State University have found that for older adults, maintaining fewer high-quality friendships is more important than having many friends. Having close friendships even outperforms having positive relationships with family members, when it comes to overall emotional and physical wellbeing.[3]

Frequency is often subject to the hands of fate and gets squashed by other factors like distance and bloated calendars. Or sometimes it just comes down to having different preferences. For example, I had a friend in Oakland who I used to see about six times a year. I talked to her about our frequency because I wanted to see her more. As it turned out, she thought our frequency was perfect. Interestingly, she said that she had recently asked another friend of hers if she wanted to hang out more frequently since they only saw each other once or twice a year. Her friend replied that she thought their frequency of one to two times per year was perfect. Oh well, you can't win 'em all.

If your frequency hopes are out of sync, you've got some decisions to make. Have a conversation about what you're each feeling and willing to offer. The person who wants more frequency either has to find a way to be happy with less, or find another friend who can be as available and dedicated as they are. The person who wants less frequency either has to step up and offer more time to demonstrate that they value the friend-ship, or they need to understand if the other person wants to step back to prioritize other people who can meet their connection needs.

In my situation, I decided that it was fine that she didn't want to hang out as frequently as I did. Instead I prioritized spending time with people in closer proximity to where I lived and who also wanted to spend more time together. My friend had a baby a couple months later and so her availability dramati-cally decreased even further. Our lives and priorities pulled us in different directions. No hard feelings. Just as people need to be emotionally available for a romantic relationship, they also need to be logistically available for platonic friendship. Or, go their separate ways.

More than 60 percent of the people I polled said they wished they could see their friends more often.[4] If you're in the same bucket, do the Frequency Assessment on the next page, then ask your friends how they feel about the frequency with which you see each other. If you both would love to connect more frequently, check out the ideas that follow for how to make that a reality.

Frequency Assessment

Get your journal and create the following lists:

• Friends you spend time with every week

• Friends you spend time with every month

• Friends you spend time with every few months or seasonally

• Friends you spend time with once or twice a year

Questions for reflection

How do you feel about the frequency with which you see your favorite friends?

Which people do you wish you saw more frequently?

What would be your favorite ways to increase your frequency with some of the people you listed?

How would your life be different if you could spend time with your favorite friends as frequently as you wanted?

Up Your Dosage

Pick two friends who you want to be closer with. Ask if they're up for increasing the frequency in your friendship. This doesn't have to mean always getting together face to face, although that's ideal. If they say yes, do whatever it takes to increase the frequency of your interactions. If you get lunch together once a month, go twice. If you normally talk on the phone once a week, spend a month talking twice a week, even if one of those calls is just ten minutes long. If you work out together once a week, throw some extra motivational texts into your weekly communication. You're going for quantity here. Try touchpoints that are easy to accomplish. See how more of a good thing can be wonderful.

If friendship was a medicine, which friends would you want more doses of? List your favorite ideas for how to get more touchpoints with them. Then tell them about it and talk about how you can both work to make it happen.

Go Together

It astounds me how frequently in college my friends and I would do our similar activities together whenever we could. Going to the grocery store or doing laundry were more than errands, they were valuable friend time when we did them together. It's funny to me how many of us do the same kinds of errands every week as adults, but how infrequently we do them together.

See which errands and tasks of yours can be done in the same time and place as your friends who have to do the same tasks. Ask your friends if they want to do them together. Spending time with friends doesn't have to come at the cost of accomplishing adult responsibilities—combining the two can actually make each task more fun and fulfilling.

Compatibility

The dictionary defines compatibility as "capable of existing together in harmony" or "a state in which two things are able to exist or occur together without problems or conflict."[1] Being compatible doesn't mean you need to be clones of each other. It means that no matter your individual personalities, you can still jibe with each other. When moments of disagreement or difference arise, you share a strong respect for, and curiosity about, each other. You support each other to feel seen, heard, and understood. Compatibility is evident when your quirks and tendencies work together instead of irritating you both. It's when you feel like kindred spirits, or like you're part of the same tribe. It's the stuff that makes being around each other so easy and enjoyable.

In friendship, there are many ways in which we can be compatible or incompatible. The five main types of compatibility I've observed are: chemistry, communication style, lifestyle, socializing style, and values. Each serves as a possible point for connection or disconnection.

Chemistry

Chemistry is usually only talked about as an element of romantic connections, but it's also a part of every other kind of relationship in our lives: family, coworkers, classmates, and friendships. A friendship obviously won't work if Person A digs Person B, but Person B feels annoyance, aversion, or indifference towards Person A. Any friendship needs chemistry in order to take off. Chemistry is when you and the other person have mutual

enthusiasm for each other. It's the "I Like You" factor—the magic that powers the bromance and the feeling of being a sister from another mister. Time flies when you're together. Chemistry is the excitement that you feel when you're around the other person; the thing that makes you want to keep being around them and you don't know why. When two people have this shared enthusiasm for each other, it can overshadow the fact that they might not share similar preferences, hobbies, jobs, or even religious or philosophical beliefs.

Communication Style

We communicate in so many ways—verbally, nonverbally, and digitally—and each of these methods holds a mix of ways that we can be compatible or incompatible. We can speak in so many ways: quickly or slowly, bluntly or diplomatically, loudly or quietly. We may be passive or direct, formal or slangy, earnest or sarcastic, vulnerable or guarded. We might physically share our thoughts in waggled eyebrows, fist pumps, high fives, and hugs, or we might sit as still and placid as a lake at dawn. We may excitedly interrupt each other every few words, or we may listen quietly and allow roomy pauses to punctuate our speech. We can blow up each other's phones with strings of emoji, bitmoji, goofy gifs, and chapter length updates about everything happening in our lives. Or we might reply with one-word questions and answers that trickle out slowly over the course of several days.

"WHAT KIND OF DOG SHOULD I GET IF I JUST NEED A CONVERSATION STARTER SO I CAN MEET PEOPLE?"

There's no right or wrong way to do any of this. What matters is that when you and your friends are keeping in touch, your communication styles pull you closer instead of driving you bananas. How we communicate is also deeply influenced by our emotional intelligence and our ability to express it. Our capacity to give each other empathy and compassion has as much to do with how we speak as it does with how we listen. We make the other person feel heard when we listen actively, summarize clearly, and offer our reflections, feelings, and perspectives.

Lifestyle

Lifestyle compatibility isn't a deal breaker but it's important enough to deserve a mention. Spending time together will be easier and more fruitful if there's crossover in the activities you each like to do and are capable of doing. At the very least, hearing about the different things your friend is into hopefully won't make you think, "Wow, that sounds like an incredible waste of time."

Lifestyle compatibility only really matters if activity-sharing is a goal of both people. For example, I don't really like hiking. I have some friends who do. After being invited on one too many hiking excursions, I had to tell a couple of them, "Hey, so, I love nature but hate hiking. I don't want you to think that I don't want to hang out with you because I never say yes when you invite me to go on your 10-mile uphill hikes in the hot sun. So, since we both love tacos, let's just get together when you're back from your trips and you can tell me all about it?" The more honest we are about our differences and expectations, the less we'll let each other down.

Socializing Style

The size of your friend circle and how you opt to engage with it is what I refer to as your socializing style. It helps to be on the same page with your friends about how many friendships you are each trying to maintain. If you only want to have two or three close friends who you spend most of your free time with, but your friend wants to be a social butterfly with several dozen "close" friends, they probably won't have enough free time in their calendar to match the amount of time that you want to spend with them.

Recently, I faced the opposite situation. I realized that I was trying to maintain too many face-to-face friendships in my local area. I didn't have the bandwidth to fit a newer acquaintance into my life, and I felt guilty turning down her invitations. So I just told her: "I have to be honest with you and admit that I'm stretched too thin. I'm not able to give each of my friends the attention they deserve, including you. I am realizing that I can only maintain a smaller social circle and so I need to take a step back. I wanted to let you know because I want to be fair to you, and so you can focus your energy on folks who have more availability to hang out with the wonderful person that you are." It was hard to say, but it took a huge weight off my shoulders. She was gracious about it and said she understood. In order for a friendship to avoid becoming a constant source of disappointment and feelings of neglect, you need to be realistic and honest about how many friendships you can actually maintain.

Similarly, it helps to be on the same page about what hangout styles work for you both. If you crave quiet one-on-one time and your friend only wants to hang out at house parties and festivals, that's probably not gonna work out. Vary your hangout formats to make sure you're not getting bored and so you both get your needs met.

Values

Although it's common for friends to share the same values, it's not necessary. The majority of the people I surveyed said that when it comes to opinions, background, beliefs, politics, religion, ideology, and worldview, they prefer for their friends to be either "a little different" (81 percent) or "meaningfully different" (17 percent) from themselves.[2] A few of their reasons for this include:

"Common ground and opinions are valuable, but I won't learn anything new or gain novel perspectives if I'm only surrounded by those exactly like mine."

"I don't like living in an echo chamber. My friends and I have many things in common, but I do actively seek out friendships with people who differ from me in background, belief, or personality type."

"I have a diverse mix of friends (including agnostic, Muslim, Catholic, Jewish, etc.). We talk about the different religions and how we have similar morals and ideologies."

"Having different people in my life means I'm challenged in a safe way."

LEARNING OPPORTUNITIES

While friendship can be easier when you're extremely similar to your friends, being different from each other increases the likelihood that you can expand each other's worldview and perspective. Friendships between people who hold dissimilar interests and viewpoints can be some of the most fruitful for learning, innovation, mental and emotional expansion, and personal growth.

For example, one of my best friends is someone who thought it was okay to say "that's so gay" when I first met him in 2001. He's a tall, hetero, white man who loves living in the country; I'm a short, queer, immigrant, Black woman who loves the city. On the surface we couldn't be more different, but he's one of the people I feel closest to in the world. I credit our compatibility to the years that we spent as housemates and the thousands of hours of conversation we shared during that time. After some intense, mutually respectful conversations, he came to under-stand why saying "that's so gay" is totally not okay. In the two decades since, we've both felt comfortable enough to ask each other questions when there was something we didn't understand or wanted to know more about with regard to how differently we experience race, gender, sexuality, and life as two very different people.

Friendships provide a safe place to be vulnerable, uncomfortable, ask "stupid questions," and genuinely contribute to each other's development, empathy, and understanding. These are friendships that live outside of the echo chambers and filter bubbles where we just have our own thoughts and experiences reflected back to us. I firmly believe that the world would be a better place if each person had at least two strong friendships with people who are remarkably different from them.

Compatibility Assessment

To be a good friend, you need to know who you are as a friend and what you're looking for in your friendships. Additionally, if you're trying to diagnose why a certain friendship just doesn't feel right, or if you're thinking of having a compatibility check-in with a friend, it helps to make sure you know yourself well before you go down that road. All of the compatibility types exist on a spectrum, so it's useful to know where you sit on that spectrum and where your friends do, too.

Head over to weshouldgettogether.com/compatibility and download the free compatibility assessment worksheets. There's no right or wrong answers — they're just a handy way to help you know yourself better, and to help you and your friends know each other better. You and your friends can even complete the worksheets together and then compare notes.

Send Platonic Love Letters

Peak friendship is getting a platonic love letter from a friend. Take some time and write down what you appreciate about your friend so much. Don't be shy about it. Be descriptive. Be effusive. Tell them what you love about them and why. Deliver it any way you know would delight them. A text message trailed by a dozen silly bitmoji? A flyer stapled to the telephone pole in front of their apartment? A handwritten letter via snail mail? A tweet tagging everyone you both know? A guitar serenade in front of all your mutual friends at happy hour? Celebrate the compatibility you share because stumbling upon it is special and rare.

Dear Jordan ~

I am so happy that we're friends! You are a shiny bright light in my life. I am constantly impressed by how creative and curious you are and how you use your imagination to express so much beauty in the world. Also, you are freakin' hilarious and you give excellent advice. If I could ever be a better friend to you, please tell me so. You deserve the best, because you are the best.

♡ yer pal,
Lee

Explore Your Differences

Have a conversation with a friend or acquaintance very different from you. Tell them what you appreciate about them as someone who has thoughts, feelings, and beliefs that are different from your own. If you're hesitant to broach the conversation, try sharing the following video with your friend as part of your invitation to talk. In Heineken's "World's Apart: An Experiment" campaign, two people who hold opposite views on the environment, abortion, and politics come together to talk and understand each other. There wasn't any screaming or insults snarled. Just two people, talking, listening, and asking questions.[3] It was respectful adult discourse over a beer, like the kinds of conversations that possibly happened in bars before the invention of radio, TV, and social media. This is not paid product placement. I legit cried when I saw this video and I believe in the premise it extols: that respectful, honest conversation between people who hold contrasting ideas can be generative, useful, and productive.

If you want to make a new friend while in pursuit of bridging divides in our society, check out the project *Hi From The Other Side* which aims to create a more compassionate world by getting people who are politically different from each other to connect as friends on a human to human level.[4]

Commitment

If frequency ensures that we show up for each other, commitment is about how we show up for each other. I might be sitting across from you physically, but be a million miles away mentally and emotionally if I'm not fully present. A strong commitment in friendship consists of all the intangible and tangible ways that we are when we say "I'll be there for you" or "I've got your back." How we show up for each other determines whether a friendship will feel balanced, supportive, trustworthy, and grounded.

Research proves—and your own real life experience probably corroborates—that friendships are more likely to survive if the friends involved share the responsibility for the friendship's maintenance equitably.[1] Whether a friendship is one day old or has been grooving for forty years, commitment is the mutual investment that powers the train and keeps it on the tracks. It's demonstrated through dedicated action and it's based on what you do, not what you say.

We show our commitment through five core behaviors: openness, caring, trust, dedication, and reciprocity. Each of these components fortifies the depth and strength of quality friendships.

Openness

Openness and its absence makes itself apparent in the ongoing ways that we include another person in our life. Openness is important at the start of a friendship and continually throughout the duration of it. No amount of "I really like you too's" will convince someone that you want to be friends if you don't take actions to make time and space for them in your life. When describing the difficulty of interacting with people who aren't open, one inter-viewee who'd relocated from the South to the West Coast quipped, "People here are cool, but they're not warm."[2]

You show your openness when you free up space in your calendar and life to incorporate the other person. It is making space for them physically and emotionally. Being emotion-ally open means that you're willing to be vulnerable, honest, and sincere with each other. Too often we forfeit depth in our conversations and replace it with "catching up," where the whole point of the conversation is to update each other about what occurred during the weeks or months in between. This can become more of an IRL news feed than an experience of real bonding. Being emotionally open requires that you move beyond a bullet list of headlines and reveal who you really are.

Caring

Mutual caring is a core component of successful friendship; it shows that you're taking the friendship seriously. It must go both ways. When only one person in a relationship is giving dedicated attention, encouragement, and nurturing to the other, that's not a friendship. It's either therapy or a life coach-client relationship and is usually accompanied by a hefty fee.

You both need to be chipping in with meaningful emotional investment and demonstration of attention and care. You can tell that you really care about someone (and that they really care about you) when you're excited about them, believe in them, and are pumped for the things they're pumped about. Caring is evident when you're there for each other as you reach for new heights or struggle through life's challenges. People who care about each other will take the time to thoughtfully challenge each other when they see a way that the other person can grow or improve.

Caring can be as small as a "You got this!" text message sent the morning of your friend's job interview, or by being at their side during a crisis. When I got appendicitis many years ago, I was living in North Florida where I had a really strong community of friends and coworkers. They were there for me through it all. The morning I was admitted to the hospital, I called into work with the bad news. That same afternoon, coworkers showed up at the hospital to see me. They tried to make me laugh and were reassuring me that I'd be okay right up until the moment that I was wheeled into surgery. Other friends visited me afterwards and brought books and gifts when it turned out that I'd have to stay at the hospital for a week due to complications.

As I reflected on that experience from my new life in the Bay Area circa 2014, I started thinking, "If I got sick or was hospitalized now, who would I call? Who, if anyone, would come see me in the hospital if I didn't show up to work in the morning?" I started asking people this simple question: "If you were at home alone and got a debilitating stomach pain in the middle of the night, who would you call?" You know what most people said? Uber or Lyft because they either don't think they'd actually be able to reach anyone in the middle of the night, or because they thought it would be too big of an imposition to bother someone late at night, even in a time of dire need. Instead of each other, it's in apps we trust. It shouldn't be that way.

Trust

Andrea Bonoir, Ph.D. and author of *The Friendship Fix*, has written that trust is built when we have the opportunity to let someone down—but we don't.[3] We need to be able to trust each other in so many ways. For example, trusting that someone is speaking honestly and being up front about what they want from friendship. We need to trust that they'll respect our right to privacy by not repeating sensitive information we've shared with them. We need to trust that they'll show up when they say they will, and won't let us down. And if they do let us down, they understand how that damages trust and they work to repair that damage.

Another aspect of trust has to do with the reliability and strength of a shared connection after a long period of separation. If you don't talk to your friend for a while and it starts to feel like your friendship is over, a lack of trust will lead you to question whether you're still friends with each other. Even if your hangouts aren't consistent, trust will allow you to comfortably believe that your connection is still tight.

Dedication

You show your dedication when you take action. Inadequate follow-through is one of the biggest friendship-related frustrations that people deal with. Sometimes it seems like we're in a famine of follow-through. In my friendship survey, a lack of dedication was named as the second biggest reason why it's hard to make and maintain friendships. Flakiness—either the other person's or one's own—gets in the way of establishing closeness.

I felt this acutely during my first year in the Bay Area when I tried to plan my own birthday dinner. I asked several of my new friends if they wanted to go to a popular Burmese restaurant. They said yes, so I made a reservation for the eight of us on a Saturday evening when everyone said they were free to celebrate. In the half hour before our scheduled reservation time, the text messages started rolling in: *Sorry I can't make it, hope you have fun...Something came up and I won't be able to come anymore...Hope you have a happy birthday, I'll be there in spirit,* etc. Only two friends actually showed up. I apologized to the restaurant for booking a large table when in fact there would only be three of us dining. I suppressed my sadness and embarrassment, and the three of us had a lovely dinner together. I tried to chalk it up as a fluke, but I've since learned that this is ridiculously common. People will RSVP Yes, then vanish like yesterday's

Snapchat messages. The prevalence of this behavior makes the act of showing up that much more powerful.

There are many ways to demonstrate your dedication to your friends. For starters, show up when you say you will. Remember the details of their lives. Call them on their birthdays, after job interviews, and when you know they're going through nerve-wracking trials and tribulations. Or on any old regular day, just let them know that they matter to you. If your memory is bad, then set a recurring reminder in your phone to check in on your friends. It doesn't matter how you remember to do it, what matters is that you do it.

Reciprocity

A clear sign of commitment is when you and your friends share a healthy balance of reciprocity. If you've ever been in a friendship where you were the only one reaching out to make plans with the other person (and it bugged the crap out of you), then you know what a lack of reciprocity feels like. Real friendship goes both ways. It doesn't mean that we have to offer each other identical invitations at an identical pace, trading interactions and favors like we're bartering on the open market. Friendship isn't a transaction. But we need to do the things that make each other feel valued. Being good at reciprocity means knowing your friend well enough to know what kinds of things will contribute to them feeling loved and valued. Gary Chapman's "5 Love Languages" doesn't only work for romantic relationships—it offers excellent tools to put into practice as a good friend, too.

Commitment Assessment

Which of your friends seems as committed to you as you are to them? Or rather, which of their specific actions make their commitment evident? Keep in mind, this is all about how you *feel*, not how someone else might want to be seen or how they'd justify their behavior.

- Grab your journal and make a list of the things your friends do that give you the feeling of being valued and connected.

- Then list the things that you do to demonstrate your commitment to your friends. Are there things you can do more of?

- Have you ever asked a friend what actions they appreciate the most as a demonstration of caring and dedication?

- How can you show up as a better friend?

Meditate on feeling gratitude for how your friends show up for you, and ask yourself how you could be showing up for them, too. Then take action to demonstrate your commitment in real life.

Reach Out

Think about the people who you'd like to have a closer friendship with. Look in all areas of your life: friends near and far in your current city, work friends, the people you bump into in the places where you spend your free time, long-distance pals, or those from your past.

Write their names on a piece of paper.

Write down the excuses that have held you back from being closer to them, and what you can do to overcome those obstacles in the future.

Then, open up and reach out. It might take some courage to let existing friends know you want a closer friendship, or to extend invitations to newer folks, but go for it. Nothing will change until you do.

Know Yourself

The best way to have a friend is to be a friend—to yourself first and foremost. It's important to know who you are and what you need in a friendship, as well as what kind of friend you're capable of being for others. Having a clear view into your own friendship DNA can be a valuable source of knowledge when you're cultivating your friendships, and when you're trying to diagnose why a certain friendship just doesn't feel right. Check out weshouldgettogether.com/seedsofconnection for tips on identifying your friendship style.

Putting it into Practice

The act of making new friends should be just as intentional as the act of dating someone new, since friendships are just as important as romantic relationships, and they often last longer. When dating, it's normal to ask someone what they're looking for in a relationship, and to have an answer to that question yourself. It's equally compassionate and efficient to be up front in the process of making friends. We usually spend more time describing what we want to share (e.g. hiking, happy hours, movie nights) than we spend describing how we want to share it. If you go to a meetup to make new friends, practice describing who you are and what you're looking for in friendship. An example:

"Hi, I'm _____. I moved here a couple years ago and plan to stay for at least a few more. I'm looking to make a couple close friends who live less than twenty minutes away and who are also staying in town for a few more years. It's important to me to hang out in person once every week or two. My ideal friend would be someone trustworthy who is into personal growth, and a good communicator who's more earnest than they are sarcastic. As a friend, I've been told that I'm a good listener, funny, and reliable. I treasure my friends and try my best to let them know on a regular basis how much I appreciate them."

In my own life, I've found that the Seeds of Connection are such reliable indicators of a friendship's likelihood to succeed that I use them as a tool to help me identify potential in a new friendship. When I am on the verge of making a new friend, I do a quick scan to notice which seeds are present or feel possible with that person. If the answer for too many of them is "nope" then I have to do the adult thing and not lead the other person on. Sure, you can take the tween's way out and ghost the other person, letting their texts go unanswered and disingenuously saying "yeah, I'd love to hang out" while you're thinking "never gonna happen." But you're an adult. Communicate like one.

Similarly, you can refer to the Seeds to Connection to evaluate the health of an existing friendship or to help you figure out what's going on when something feels off. If a friendship seems to be going south, scan over the Seeds of Connection to hone in on exactly why so you can be specific when you talk to your friend about it.

Proximity, frequency, and commitment are about choice and action. Compatibility is up to chance. You get to decide which seeds you'll fertilize when trying to create a brand new friendship, or, when you see that an existing friendship is going awry. Try it in your own life. It will give you an interesting answer the next time someone asks you what you've been up to lately and you get to reply with "cultivating better friendships" instead of something generic like "keeping busy."

Another thing: try not to let this list stress you out. The Seeds of Connection may seem like a huge checklist of things that all have to be perfect in order for a friendship to work, but that's not necessarily so. Some seeds matter a lot when you're young. Some matter more as the years go on. Some take precedence when you're going through big life stuff, or in certain seasons of your life. Keep them in mind as you're pulling new friends into your life and deepening existing friendships, or when you're KonMari-ing your life and over-enthusiastically decluttering your social circle.

Keep an open mind and heart. Read on for inspiration on how to keep your friendship garden growing into whatever you want it to be, whether that's a spontaneous blend of heirloom wildflowers, a tightly manicured English garden, an intentionally spare Zen garden, or thick and heady tropical jungle. Next, we'll tackle the four most common obstacles for adult friendship and delve into creative strategies for how to overcome them.

FINDING BELONGING IN A HYPERMOBILE WORLD

Millions of us move every year for work, love, family, and adventure. Strong inward and outward migration is a characteristic of exciting big cities. According to *Bloomberg*, New York, Chicago, and Los Angeles suffer from the highest outward migration rates in the nation.[1] And according to *SF Gate*, more people leave the Bay Area, where I live, than any other region in the nation.[2] The highly transient nature of big cities leaves a lot of people I've interviewed feeling frustrated and lacking a sense of community. They want to make friends—but the emotional investment and effort hardly seems worth it since they, or their desired friends, are probably going to be moving on soon.

Most of the people I've met in the Bay Area arrived in the last several years, and many of them don't plan on sticking around. Around 50 percent of Bay Area residents, a number that's been rising over the last several years, are planning on moving away in the next few years.[3] In a short amount of time, I've watched a lot of the friends I made here become a part of that statistic. They moved to other cities for multiple reasons: to live somewhere more affordable, to be closer to family or communities from another time in their past, or to start families in a place that will be easier financially and socially. I discovered that if you move to a fabulous world-class city filled with interesting people—and you realize that you lack close friends there—solving that problem can be a daunting task because the targets keep moving, *literally*. Having the freedom to start over at any time in a new place also means that you have the freedom to step into isolation and placelessness when you land somewhere where no one knows you or cares what happens to you.

I've been a part of the wave of coming and going myself. In the last seven years, I've lived in three different states and had six different jobs. My life has been a nearly constant process of re-adjusting and reorienting myself. As I've moved to new cities, I've had lots of opportunities to think about how to make new friends and build community in unfamiliar places. For me, connecting with people in deep, life-enriching ways is the point of being alive. I'd always found it easy to build strong, long-lasting friendships—until I moved to the Bay Area that is, which was a phenomenon that puzzled me. It's a huge part of the reason I wrote this book.

This stuff matters. Research shows that positive social relationships add years to your life and keep you healthier while you live it.[4] Turning down friendships just because we don't expect to stay in our current cities forever is like saying, "No thanks, I prefer to die early." Why rob yourself of the benefits of human

connection, however fleeting? A lot of us spend more time thinking about living somewhere else than we do figuring out how to feel more belonging in the place we already live.

But what if we did the opposite instead? What if we treated our short time here the way we do when we make a spontaneous friend on a trip in a new place—where, instead of avoiding them since neither of us is staying in that city or town forever, we dive right in and we dive deep? It certainly didn't stop us during high school or college, when we knew for certain that we'd all be moving on after a few years. What if, when it came to friendship, we treated every new address as if it were our last? What if we opted for high-intensity short-term friendships where, instead of deciding it's not worth it, we said, "We're only going to be here for a minute, so let's make it amazing."

In this chapter, we'll explore how hypermobility can lead us to subconsciously subvert our innate urge to connect. Then we'll examine how we can break free from the limiting beliefs and behaviors that enable that tendency. We'll come face to face with the #NoNewFriends phenomenon faced by so many people who have the courage to be new in town. We'll interrogate why our neighborhoods and apartment hallways are devoid of the constant flow of friends and easy companionship that our favorite TV shows portray. And we'll delve into strategies for how to make the most of what you've got for however short of a time you get to have it.

BE HERE NOW

The social ties we fail to make cost us much more than the U-Hauls we roll in and out of town in. When we experience a drought in positive social ties, it can color our opinion of whole cities, or even entire chapters of our lives. The constant in-flow and out-flow of people in big city environments can overwhelm the senses, leading to an intensified version of the decision paralysis that we might feel when we encounter forty different kinds of cereal at the supermarket.

Eddie, a former colleague of mine compared this to the throwaway attitude that accompanies life in a culture with an overabundance of everything. "People treat each other like they're disposable," he said. "You swipe past people on dating apps and you swipe past them when you see them in real life. I hate it but it's even affected me."[1] He recounted a story about walking down the street in San Francisco and thinking that he recognized a guy who he met back home in Atlanta. Even though his girlfriend encouraged him to go say hi, he shrugged it off. The next time he saw the guy from a distance, he ignored him again. By the third time he saw the guy, Eddie had to beat down the feeling inside that was preventing him from reaching out. "I literally had to fight this voice in my head that was saying 'No, don't do it, what's the point, it doesn't matter.'"

What was stopping him? The fact that Eddie knows he's planning to move back to Atlanta. What helped him get up the gumption to reach out was taking a deep breath and connecting

to a feeling of possibility. "We might have mutual friends back home, or we might become friends here, then both end up living in Atlanta again," he surmised. So he walked over to say hi. They had a good chat and made plans to see each other again. When they hung out, they had a great time. Eddie's decision to accept the fact that he was right here, right now, paid off.[1]

When we're faced with an overabundance of choices, the stress can prevent us from taking any action at all. Unfortunately, the constantly fluctuating population of people around us can induce the same type of stress. It can prevent us from even trying to catch a single person's attention. It can feel too big. We can feel too small. The trick is to feel the discomfort and do it anyway. It's easier if you start with a familiar stranger. Here's a story about two of my own:

Lucas and his old dog Cooper walk slowly up and down my block twice every day. We'd often pass by each other outside on the sidewalk. Slowly, we graduated from "strangers you ignore" to "strangers you give that funny half-smile to," then "strangers you smile and wave at," and then finally "Hey, we should probably introduce ourselves since we see each other all the time." Turns out he's a pretty cool guy who lives four doors down. An invitation to swing by any time to play music and hang out followed. When the plum tree in my yard was overflowing with fruit one day, I shared an armload with him as he and Cooper were passing by and we had a good laugh about it. I couldn't believe we waited so long to say hello.

I've also had success making a new friend at my bus stop, where I see the same other commuters every morning at the same time. Graduating from bus stop friends to hangout friends was easy with one of my new friends, Alex, who always returned my "good morning" greeting with a chatty reply. After several bus stop chats, we graduated to going on walks and sharing home-cooked meals. We're both excited to now have a new friend who lives less than a five minute walk away. If you're seeing the same people every time you commute, it's pretty obvious that you live in close proximity to each other, so why not start there?

Talk to Strangers

Are you afraid to talk to your familiar strangers? Why? Of course you need to be careful, but make sure you're not blocking new friendships by guarding yourself against dangers that aren't really there.

Chances are, most of your familiar strangers are as nice as you are. With as hard as it can be to schedule time to see friends face to face, you might as well start with the people who are already right there in front of you.

Pick two people that you see on a regular basis and who seem pretty friendly: they can be people who commute on public transit on the same schedule that you do, or neighbors in your apartment or on your block. The next couple times you see them, strike up a conversation. Introduce yourself if you haven't before. Ask how they like living in the neighborhood, or if they have made friends with other neighbors in the area. Let them know that you've been trying to get to know more people in the building/neighborhood and ask if they want to go for a walk or hang out sometime. (If none of these prompts feel comfortable, then by all means, say what feels natural to you.) It's no guarantee that every person you meet will become your new BFF, but even if it doesn't work out, at least you'll both up feeling more like friendly neighbors and less like total strangers.

MAKe IT WORK

Sometimes the people right in front of you are those who happened to get hired around the same time you did. I've been lucky to have made lifelong friends at some of the jobs I've had. In those situations, the border between work and non-work was fluid, irrelevant, or otherwise non-existent. At other jobs, I barely made more than casual acquaintances. The border between work and non-work was strong and nearly clasped shut. Neither of these scenarios is my ideal. I like to keep pretty clear boundaries between work and the rest of my life, but occasionally when I make a true friend at work, I flex the line between those two parts of my life to let more joy and connection in. I'm lucky to have a couple of friends like that in my office job right now. We've laughed and cried together, been there to support each other through hard days, and had some heart-to-hearts that really cemented our friendship. Still, we had never hung out outside of the office.

Shortly after the movie *Crazy Rich Asians* opened, three of us decided to go see it after work on a Friday. The gentle ease of our work friendship translated seamlessly to our outing at the movie theater. Our conversations were playful and relaxed, and being together on this microscopic adventure made me feel closer to both of them. We joked about the shockingly large selection of snacks in the concession area (samosas at the movies?!) and then gorged on popcorn and cookie dough ice cream. We gushed about the film afterwards and shared a couple personal stories about how parts of the storyline paralleled experiences from our own lives. By the time we were hugging goodbye, it was pretty late and I wanted to get home quickly. Instead of my usual bus ride, I decided to take a Lyft. The driver, who I'll call Isaac, arrived in a clean black Camry a few minutes later. He greeted me from the front seat with a friendly hello and a wave from behind a brightly knit yarmulke fastened to the top of his head.

Both of us in buoyant moods, we chatted energetically about how our evenings were going so far. A few minutes later, as we sped past the lumbering sparkle of a shiny tech company commuter bus, Isaac made a comment about how obnoxious he thought those private buses are. We talked about the pros and cons of the buses—the way they help keep cars off the road, but how they also contribute to class division and detract from the development of a more robust public transportation system for everyone. Then he dropped a bomb on me. He said that he'd never want to work for a company like that … even though he's a computer programmer.

Wait. What? I asked why he was driving for Lyft if he's a programmer. There's no immediately clear reason why someone with a skillset that lucrative would need to drive for extra money. Isaac explained that he works alone at home—and has been working that way for the majority of the last thirty years. Working alone has its benefits; no one is looking over his shoulder and he gets to make his own hours. But there are two main downsides: it leaves him feeling socially isolated, and it strains his eyes because staring at a computer screen means he is always focusing his eyes on things at a short distance.

A few years ago he started driving for Lyft part time. His voice was beaming with a smile as he explained how and why he loves it so much. He said that driving a morning shift from 7 to 9 a.m. wakes him up and gets him going. He loves to watch the sun come up, and driving lets him get a peek into different neighborhoods that he'd otherwise never see. It gives his eyes a chance to focus at a distance and witness the rest of the world waking up too. When he sits down at his computer at 9 a.m., he's refreshed and ready to get to work. The best part about driving, he said, is that it gives him a chance to talk to people and really connect with them in a way that his workday could never provide. He later decided to add an evening shift a few times a week. He doesn't drive for the money; he drives for the human connection.[1]

The ride was smooth, but in the back seat my head was spinning with a major case of deja vú. Isaac is the second computer engineer I've spontaneously met who has told me that he's a part-time driver primarily because it reduces his feelings of social isolation. Both guys said the best thing about driving is that it gives them a chance to connect with people and have great conversations.

The other driver, Aaron, was a participant at one of my *Better Than Small Talk* gatherings. For Aaron too, the main benefit of being a driver is that his rides with strangers lead to much deeper conversations than what he typically experiences with his coworkers or when socializing with people he knows.[2] In the fleeting container of an 18-minute road trip, these two are courageously reaching for, and finding, the kind of connection that's missing in other parts of their lives. Isaac, Aaron, and the riders who keep them on the road have turned part-time taxis into intimacy shuttles. They are using the relative anonymity of their temporary proximity to have conversations about what really matters in their lives, despite the moment's ephemerality, or maybe because of it. It's like a G-rated emotional intelligence version of *Taxicab Confessions*.

I've heard of some pretty creative ways to combat social isolation, but getting an unnecessary second job might take the cake. There's something very sweet and sincere about their strategy, though, and I found it hard to stop thinking about their stories. Isaac and Aaron: two programmers driving people around in their free time, using their creative problem-solving skills to engineer human connection into super-connected lives that have failed to deliver it.

Work It Out

Do you have a couple of friends at work that you really like but haven't hung out with outside of work yet? Go ahead and ask them if they want to get together. The easiest times are likely to be right before or right after you're both going to be at work since you know that you're going to be near the same location at the same time. Or take it a step further and make plans to do something together on a non-work day. When you make plans, follow through. And when you hang out, don't just talk about work-related gossip. Get to know each other as people who have entire lives and identities beyond your roles at work. Grab a few conversation starters from the list at the back of this book to kick things off and see where the conversation takes you.

Mo New Friends

Nina never had any problems making friends.[1] College provided her with a tight-knit friend group that even got together after graduation every Labor Day weekend—until marriage and families and cross-country moves scattered everyone across time zones and squeezed their calendars shut. Her first job out of college was at an accounting firm in Philadelphia where she and her new-hire cohort became fast friends. Having recurring access to each other at seasonal weeklong trainings and being on a career path moving at the same pace helped her and her coworkers develop a sense of trust and camaraderie. Despite moving away several years ago, she still travels to visit her accounting friends a few times a year. However, her friendship experience started going downhill after two big city moves.

A stint in Baltimore left her and her then-boyfriend feeling strangely isolated. "That was the first time that I realized how challenging it is to make new friends as an adult if you're not making them at work," she told me. Baltimore was tough. "It seemed like if you hadn't been born and raised in the suburbs of Baltimore, and gone to school with all these people, you were always going to be on the periphery because everyone had thirty-five friends who they've known their whole lives. It wasn't that they didn't want to invite us, but we would always be an afterthought. We always had to carry the relationship. That wasn't a bad thing, per se, but it was different."

Nina and her boyfriend questioned whether their lack of friends was their own fault. They wondered if, by blaming the Baltimore-native dynamics, they were making excuses for not trying hard enough to make friends. They struggled with it and chalked it up to bad luck. After they split up, Nina thought she might strike gold with a new life in San Francisco.

The Bay Area seemed like it might provide a softer landing. A few of her acquaintances from high school and college were already there. "Everyone was excited that I was moving to town. But once I'd been out here for a couple months and wasn't new anymore, everybody was over it." It was difficult to even get a coffee date with any of her acquaintances after a while. She had thought it would be easier to find new friends in SF because of how the city seems to draw all different kinds of people to it. Its reputation for creativity, openness, and energy appealed to her.

"While people have been a lot friendlier here, it's still really hard. It's been weirdly challenging to actually make and maintain friendships and to break into some kind of group. It feels like everyone's already established themselves." She couldn't even get a break at work. Her new job was teamless, and while her role allowed her to talk to people, it was never the same group of people. It required all the effort of being social with none of the benefits of continuity.

Nina even tried joining a social and philanthropic organization for unmarried professional women between the ages of twenty-one and thirty-five. "I hit it off well with these twenty-two- and twenty-three-year-old girls who are new to the city, fresh out of college and ready to start the adult chapter of their

life. But I'm almost thirty-two years old, and I don't want to go bar-hopping by the Marina. That's not where I am in my life right now. When I do meet women who are my age, they're not saying, 'Hey, let's be friends! Let's do something this weekend.' They're like, 'Oh, um, yeah. I've been here for eight years. I live with my boyfriend. I have my fifteen girlfriends. Nice to meet you. Have a nice night.'

She put herself out there repeatedly, with similarly fruitless results. "I took a woodworking class thinking that would be a good way to make friends. And sure, I can banter with the people who are at the same table as me when we're working on a project. But it's not like we get to a moment where we're all like, 'Okay, now let's exchange numbers and hang out all the time.' More likely,

they say, 'Yeah, hi, here's my buddy. This is fun. See you later. Bye.'
It's tough!'"

Nina has found that being single and new in town can be a
first-class ticket to the thirtysomething friendship desert. She has
to fight the urge to give up and be antisocial. She admits that
sometimes when it's too hard, she surrenders to staying at home
with a bottle of wine and Netflix. She figures she'll just wait to hang
out with friends when she can fly out and visit them in Boulder,
Montreal, or wherever else they've moved on to.

Ironically, she has seen the same closed-off attitudes surface in
her own long-term friend group. "It's not like the easy openness of
college at all. Every once in a while a couple people in my Philly
friend group will jokingly say #NoNewFriends. And I'm like, why
do we feel like we don't want new people to join our group? I don't
know what that kind of protective attitude is about. I don't want
to be part of the problem."

After two years of trying to make friends in San Francisco,
Nina said she's made exactly one new, genuine friend. Despite
all her struggles, she's doing better than a lot of people. According
to a recent study conducted for Evite, a party-planning website
where you can send and manage free invitations, the average
American hasn't made one new friend in the last five years. Over
80 percent of the 2,000 people surveyed said that they felt enduring
friendships are hard to find and keep. The number one reason why
friendships fizzle out? Relocation.[2]

Online articles abound about how to make friends when
you're new in town. Their advice runs the gamut from run-of-the-
mill tips like shop local, go to meetups, join a faith community,

attend group workout classes, volunteer, reach out to friends-of-friends, or join a book club, to out-of-the-ordinary tips like borrow a dog and go to a dog park, attend living room concerts, join a running club, keep a spreadsheet with details about all the people you meet and schedule coffee every week. One of the best pieces of advice I've ever heard on this topic centered less on *what* to do, and more on *how* to do it. Namely, don't go it alone.

Frankie moved from the Midwest to Oakland for grad school and didn't know anyone when she arrived.[3] Her first year was pretty lonely, spent just going to classes and studying at home in the tiny studio apartment behind her landlord's house. After moving into an apartment that she shared with a few other people, she found her first social group through one of her roommates. At first she didn't connect much with this set of friends-of-a-friend, but in time, they grew closer. Frankie didn't expect to stay in the area after grad school, so she wasn't invested in forming close friendships.

That all changed once she made up her mind to stay. She realized she wanted to build stronger friendships and that she'd need to put in the time and effort to make it happen. She got involved in a basketball league that ended up being a consistent part of her life in the ten years that followed. Her league community has been a reliable source of close friends, casual friends, and friendly acquaintances—they practice together, attend birthday parties, go to events, celebrate each other's life milestones like new babies and marriages, and even care for each other after loved ones pass away. She acknowledges that her athletic community might be unusually close, and that not everyone plays a sport that can serve as a gateway to connection.

POSSIBILITY OF RECONNECTION

HANG OUT ALONE

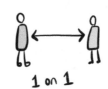

1 on 1

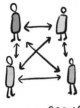

SMALL GROUP

PARTY

The court wasn't her only link to friendship and community, though. Reflecting on how she was able to rack up the necessary hours to build friendships that stick, Frankie praised the small-group outing—doing something new and novel with an intentionally small group of people.

"A good example of this is based on how I like the band Thao and The Get Down Stay Down," Frankie explained, "I've gone to see Thao shows with different friends, sometimes one-on-one, and sometimes in small groups. But the best in terms of making friends was when I went with a small group, like four people. Because then every time Thao was coming back to play a show, there was a higher likelihood that one of us would hear about it, and then that person reached out to the other three people to see if we heard about it, or to see if we all wanted to go together. The more people that share a common point of reference for an experience, the more people you have who will reach out to you to reconnect about that thing you have in common."

A small group allows you to form memories with each member of the group. Shared memories multiply the chances that someone will prompt the others to re-engage. Reconnection is more likely to happen, since it can come from more sources, and each person has a connection with everyone else. It's also less work because you don't have to exert as much energy maintaining three separate friendships all by yourself. Everyone in the group is by proxy helping everyone else maintain their friendships too.

Since I usually opt for one-on-one hangouts with my friends, Frankie's story was eye-opening for me. I realized I had been making it harder on myself than I needed to. It's not that I've never hung out in small groups before. It's that I never thought of specifically utilizing the small group format to catalyze friend-making because it's more efficient and more generative.

A young man named Bader that I interviewed in Berkeley uses the same small-group strategy, and purposely uses the opportunity to play platonic-matchmaker for his friends by introducing people who have a lot in common. For example, he recently connected two friends who were both musicians and who share a similar critical analysis of representation within the music industry. After the group hangout, they each separately thanked him for pulling off such a well-orchestrated gathering. His friends had connected splendidly and they each appreciated Bader more for making it happen.[4] You can ask your friends and acquaintances to do this for you, too.

In my friendship survey, the majority of participants said their ideal hangout format would be a small group of three to six people. When they're with friends, most said they usually eat, drink, and go to movies or concerts. Pretty straightforward. More interestingly, while not necessarily dissatisfied with their hangout routines, most people said they crave more variety in how they spend time with friends. Many wished that they hung out in different size groups or that they did a broader variety of activities together, such as learning new skills, taking small trips, or spending time in nature[5]—which I really hope they get around to. Research proves that doing more unique activities rewards people with greater feelings of closeness than they're getting from sharing nachos and margaritas.

In the 2018 study, titled "Sharing Extraordinary Experiences Fosters Feelings of Closeness," researchers at Cornell University discovered that when people who don't know each other very well share an out-of-the-ordinary experience together, it bonds them much faster than doing a staid activity.[6] The more extraordinary the experience, the stronger the bond. Why? Because in an intense situation people are distracted by the extraordinariness of the details and less focused on any discomfort that might come from interacting with someone they don't know very well. Novelty is like an inoculation against social awkwardness.

If you've been thinking about switching up your hangout formation or friendship activities, there's a good chance that you're not the only one who is secretly wishing for it. So extend the invitation. Plan some off-the-beaten-path outings and invite a few #NewFriends to join you.

Be the Captain of a Tiny Ship

In *The Art of Gathering*, Priya Parker describes aimless gatherings with too-chill leaders as "skipperless ships."[7] When you pull a group of people together, you have an opportunity to make it something special. Embrace the power of pulling together a small group and trying various experience experiments. Remember that one of the best things you can do to ensure success is to pick an unusual activity that you and your friends haven't done before.

Pull together:
• Someone you know well
• Someone you know a little bit
• Someone you barely know at all but really like

Then pick an unconventional activity to do together:
• Take the strangest cooking class you can find
• Go to an exhibit for an unfamiliar artist
• Attend a lecture by an unfamiliar speaker on an unusual topic at an unfamiliar place
• Go to an art class or workshop that's new for all of you, like pinhole camera making, ceramics, puppet-making, screen-printing or glass-blowing
• Be a spectator at a game that none of you is familiar with
• Go to a meetup for something you've never heard of

• Get off the train somewhere you've never been and take a neighborhood discovery walk

• Go to a concert for a band none of you has seen live before

• Take a dance class that none of you have tried before, e.g. Afrobeat, Bhangra, Pole, Zydeco

• Volunteer together to help an organization that none of you are familiar with

• Visit a music shop and play around on unusual instruments

• Go to a protest or demonstration, especially if you've never attended one before

• Check out a festival or convention that is unlike any you've ever been to before, e.g. AlienCon, Sand Sculpture Competition, Pun-Off Competition, Tattoo Convention, Tiny Living Festival, etc.

GET COMFORTABLE

Take a deep breath, look into your memory vault, and think about where you usually are when you spend time with the people that you feel closest to in the world. My guess would be that you spend a lot of the time at one of your homes. The people who answered my friendship survey said their hangouts look like this:

Acquaintances: ~90 percent outside of the home
Friends: ~80 percent outside of the home
Close Friends: ~70 percent *inside* the home[1]

If we think someone's safe enough to call a "friend", why don't we invite them over more often? Is it because going out is more fun? If going out is so great, why do so many of us choose to stay home when we hang out with our closest pals? One reason might be, as a survey respondent said, "The intimate setting of home is a great way to spend an extended period of time with someone without feeling the pressure to move onto a new activity or spend more money."

There is another reason why I think we stay at home more with our closest friends. It's the same reason why I think we should stay home more often with our not-yet-close friends who we want to be closer to. When you're somewhere you feel at ease, you put others at ease, and when you're both at ease, it's easy to connect in more authentic ways. Inviting someone in is literally and figuratively inviting them *in*.

Maybe noisy cafes and interrupting waitstaff make intimate conversations easy for you, but they don't for me. If you're not developing the closeness and intimacy you wish you had with your friends, consider whether the spaces where you spend time together might be unintentionally resulting in outcomes that you don't want.

Just think for a minute about the way we use the phrase "personal space." It's space for the person that you are. If you never invite someone into the spaces that are a reflection of who you truly are, like your home, what does that say about how much you're willing to let them know about you as a person? Some of us know more about which coffee shop has the best ambiance, or which bar makes the best cocktails, than we know about the ingredients that make up the person we're talking to.

"THIS PLACE HAS A GREAT HAPPY HOUR!"

In high school, like many American teens in the '90s, I often hung out at my friends' houses after school. Being teenagers with limited access to freedom or privacy, we usually just hung out in my friends' rooms. Even if it was our first time hanging out outside of school, it wasn't weird at all to just go hang out in their room. It was so simple. We'd just sit on a bed or the floor, flip through magazines, and talk. We might talk about how the day went, reminisce about some adventure we had the previous weekend, or complain about something crappy in our lives. It was laid-back, comfortable, and personal.

In college we lived in dorms, slept in close quarters, and spent lots of time together in our most homey spaces: bedrooms, bathrooms, shared study spaces. If, as adults, we only spend time with potential friends in spaces that are inoculated of any personal essence, like coffee shops, stores, bars, and restaurants, what are we communicating? With the distance we put between the other person and our personal physical space, are we silently saying, "I don't want to get too close to you. I don't want you to know more about me and the environmental clues about what makes me up as a person. I prefer to keep a distance between you and the artifacts of my personal life that might expose more about who I really am. I prefer to see you in tightly controlled, external, and highly curated experiences, instead of in the raw, sometimes messy, sometimes uncomfortable real moments of my life."

For many, the hesitation is more externally driven. Multiple survey respondents commented that they want to invite people over to their house more often but don't because they're worried that their home isn't nice enough, welcoming enough, or comfortable enough. They said things like:

"I wish that we could hang out at each other's houses but I'm too insecure about imposing on them or not being a good host."

"I'd like my home to be more welcoming, cleaner, etc. I never seem to have time and/or money to make it the way I want it."

"If I had a bigger home I'd have people over more often."[2]

In the past twenty years, I've lived with dozens of house-mates in configurations ranging from a 2-person flat, to a 7-person shared house, to an intentional community with over 100 residents. I can completely relate to feeling self-conscious about having people over and worrying that your space is not welcoming or comfortable enough because you don't have control over what happens in your home. When I lived with people who were a little antisocial, I didn't want their iciness to make my friends feel unwelcome, so I didn't invite friends to come over that much. I felt especially hesitant to have people over when I had roommates who would leave huge messes all over the place. I didn't want to be judged for that. I censored my own invitations and let my worries about the shared space not being nice enough stop me from inviting people over.

But is this really something we need to worry about? Have you ever been invited to someone's house and immediately walked out the door because their stack of mail on the counter or cereal bowl in the sink was just too intolerable to handle? I doubt it. We need to stop judging ourselves so harshly and thinking that we can only "host" people when our homes look like an Instagram photo with thousands of likes. Just invite people in. Sit anywhere. Your decorations don't matter. You're not "entertaining," you're spending time with someone you really like. That's what matters. Trust me, this is something I try to remind myself all the time.

I've noticed something else about this that has come with getting older. When I was younger, having people over was just "hanging out." But somewhere during my thirties, having people over turned into "hosting." What's that about? This isn't a late night talk show. Why am I "hosting" all of a sudden? It's just a vocabulary change, but words come with their own baggage. This is one that I think deserves some scrutiny. "Hosting" and "entertaining" are words that fancy lifestyle magazines and HGTV makeover shows use to describe having people over—usually while they're redesigning a deck or remodeling a den-kitchen combo complete with pool table, twelve-seat sectional, and wet bar. I for one feel a completely different type of energy when I use those words. Entertaining and hosting are words that fill me with a sense of pressure, anxiety, and expectations about how things "should" be. Something about those words robs the focus away from feelings, emotions, and interactions, and puts the focus instead on the structure, style, and execution.

Think about it this way. In real life, when you've been at a best friend's house having a heart-to-heart about something that really matters in your life, did you get up and formally thank them for "entertaining" you when it was over? I doubt it. That would probably come off as clinical and transactional.

When I was lucky enough to live next door to my best friend Rae in Seattle, we spent a ton of time at each other's houses— dirty dishes in the sink, bare feet on the couch, and all. We were only acquaintances when I first moved across the street from her, but the time spent talking on the couch and around the dinner table is what produced the conversations that turned us into best friends. One of my favorite things about our friendship is its easy casual intimacy. I firmly believe that a key reason why we maintain it even after all these years is because we spent nearly all of our friendship-building time together at one of our homes (usually me at her place). I don't think we used any variation of the words "host" or "entertain" to describe what we were doing even once. It was way simpler than that:

> *"Hey, I'm home now, come on over."*
> *"It was so good to see you."*

"Thanks for dinner, next time I'll cook."
"Sweet, I'll swing by tomorrow after work."

Bars and restaurants are fun, but they're also expensive, noisy, and full of interruptions. I think it's time to start inviting people over much more often, especially when we feel self-conscious about things not being "nice enough." In fact, if you're worried about potential friends judging you for not living somewhere that looks like the set of a photo shoot, I'd like to offer you a challenge:

- invite people over when your house is just a little bit messy
- purposely leave a few dirty dishes in the sink
- or leave your pile of mail on the counter
- or leave your basket of unfolded laundry in the living room

If such a minor mess disqualifies you as a friend, you probably don't want to be friends with that person anyway. And if it doesn't bug them, then see, you had nothing to worry about. If they like you anyway, it means they really like you. Don't try to be those immaculately curated lifestyle and home decor influencers whose photos are styled by professionals and shot on a set. You be you. Tell people to come over. Let them see you, the real you, in your real environment. If there's a friend or acquaintance in your life that you'd like to be closer to, invite them to spend time with you in your home a little earlier than you normally would. It might be awkward, or it might be surprisingly comfortable. The mere fact that you're both in one of your actual personal spaces might have a positive impact on the way you relate to each other. The depth of your connection might immediately transform simply because you're more likely to feel comfortable and open when you're in a place where you already feel at ease.

To crank down any nervousness you might feel about the imperfections of your home or the pressure to be a perfect "host," try what I did the last time I invited Tracy, a newish friend, to come over and hang out. Text the other person ahead of time and say, "Feel free to wear sweats if you want to be super comfortable because I am definitely ultra casual right now. Let's keep this easy and relaxing :)." I got home from work, changed into my sweats, and left the dishes in the sink instead of frantically rushing to make everything look perfect. When I said jokingly, "Thanks for not judging me for my dirty dishes in the sink," Tracy laughed and replied, "I'm so glad they're there. It makes me feel more at home because this is what my sink looks like." I always want my friends to feel at home when they're around me. I've learned that one of the best ways to do that is to bring them there.

Get Real, Get Comfortable

Think about spending time together in a space that feels more intimate or personal for you, a space that might facilitate the kinds of conversations that result in greater connection and bonding. Switch up how you normally do things.

If you always go out, stay in. If you always stay in, go out. Whether your norm is to stay in or go out, also try spending some time in nature together (bonus: it's free). Get together in a new way. Give a budding friendship the kind of room it can grow in.

Tackle a To-Do Together

Laura Parker, creator of Transforming Loneliness, an online summit that explores the many facets of loneliness, says one of her favorite friendship-building ideas is to invite someone over to share a task like gardening or cooking. "It allows for gentle spaces and easy silences that break up the conversation at a natural pace. It just feels more relaxed."[3] Conversations like these have a different energy than the sitting-upright-in-a-chair conversations that happen when you're in a coffee shop surrounded by strangers who can't help but eavesdrop because they're sitting one foot away.

If there's something you've been wanting to get done, but you've put it off to prioritize socializing instead, combine the two. Clean out your closet, repot your plants, organize the cabinets, sort through old magazines or art supplies, organize your desk, do your meal prep. Just add "hang out with a friend" to the list at the same time.

SETTLE IN

The way we relate to each other in big American cities hasn't changed a lot over the last eighty years.[1] That's because our cities are still designed in many of the same ways that they were back then (minus the amazing streetcar networks). American cities are rarely designed for their residents' greatest psychological or emotional enjoyment. Dense urban areas hurl us into the path of people we don't know, day in and day out. On the flip side, geography and traffic keep us at a frustrating distance from the people that we do know and want to be near to. It's like a game of pinball, where we're the ball being batted around by the shoulders and elbows of strangers rushing past, and every so often we score a point by zipping across the path of a real friend.

After we get worn down by the hustle and bustle of the city, we retreat. Some of us resort to avoiding other people and adopt a cagey skepticism that's attempting to keep us emotionally or physically safe. Or, we run away from downtown. If you start ambling around residential or suburban areas, there is a different though equally sad picture. We're free to walk without being pushed around, but that's only because there is rarely anyone else walking, and very few places to walk to. Whether the sidewalks are crowded or deserted, our cities compel us to walk through the world alone, and we call that independence.

The design of our cities and their accompanying walks-cores impact our waning access to friendship more than you might imagine. Walk Score has scored the walkability of 121 cities in the US, Canada, and Australia with populations greater than 200,000. A Walk Score defines how easy or difficult it is for residents to reach amenities such as parks and grocery stores on foot in less than thirty minutes. A score of 0-24 would mean that residents are abysmally car-dependent while a score of 90-100 is considered a Walker's Paradise. The average score is 49 which means a neighborhood is "somewhat walkable" and some amenities can be reached by foot. Neighborhoods that are labeled "Very Walkable" and "Walker's Paradise" are unlikely to ever require a car.[2] Some of the nation's most walkable neighborhoods include New York's Union Square, San Francisco's Chinatown, and Boston's North End.[3] Residents in more walkable neighborhoods weigh less, report having better health, happiness, and wellbeing—and yes, more friends, too.[4]

In a famous study, urban designer Donald Appleyard compared a street in San Francisco that had light car traffic (2,000 passing vehicles per day) with another that had heavy car traffic (16,000 vehicles per day). Residents on the street with higher traffic had one-third as many friends and one-half as many acquaintances as residents on the low-traffic street.[5]

Our cities are good at concentrating the apparatus of modern capitalism, but they are generally terrible at helping us live healthy, friend-filled lives that move at a human pace. I agree with the experts who say that the best recipe for friendship would be structural, ensuring that everyone lives in well-designed, safe, spontaneity-enhancing neighborhoods with walkscores of 90 or above. Walkable neighborhoods where an intergenerational mix of community members can bump into each other while they carry out the most frequent journeys of daily life (work, school, play, food, etc.) are the best way for people to see each other. In a well-designed neighborhood where your friends also live, you don't have to try hard to see them, it just happens.

The issue is that a millions of people don't have access to the limited stock of housing that is embedded in our nation's most walkable, amenity-filled, park-filled neighborhoods. Until zoning laws and public policy radically change to support the creation of many more neighborhoods like them, this will continue to be the case. But that shouldn't stop us from doing what we can to develop and maintain strong friendships right on our own streets, stoops, balconies, and backyards.

It won't always be easy. A third of Americans have never even interacted once with any of their neighbors. One possible reason is that people don't trust each other as much as they used to. Journalist Meaghan McDonogh reported in the *Boston Globe* that in the mid-1980s about 50 percent of Americans said they trusted other people. Now, only about 30 percent of Americans say they trust other people, even though the national crime rate has fallen by at least half.

I suspect that as technology has either limited our interactions to the circle of people we already know, or habituated us to lives of constant curation, we've become less tolerant of, and more suspicious of, any interaction that is a) spontaneous and b) involves a stranger. This leads us to regard the strangers we're closest in proximity to with hesitation and mistrust.

Neighbors

THE GREAT AMERICAN MYSTERY

How comfortable would you feel knocking on your neighbor's door? How would you feel if they knocked on yours? If the thought of interacting with your neighbors is off-putting, ask yourself what you lose by maintaining this unnecessary distancing. What might you gain instead?

A piece of pop culture irony that always gets me is how the media we love rarely reflects the lives we live. You ever notice how on TV shows about friends (e.g. *Friends, Seinfeld, How I Met Your Mother, That 70s Show, Euphoria*) the characters have near constant access to each other because they either live together or they live close enough to walk through the door at any moment? Most of our lives don't look like that, in part because we don't let them.

In psychology, peak experiences are described as moments that give us intense and transcendent feelings of happiness, fulfillment with self, and fulfillment with life.[6] One of my peak experiences was a subtle one. It wasn't even a singular event. It happened twice, and each time lasted a couple years. It was the simple circumstance of getting to live with daily access to a best friend. With Balthazar, it was when we were housemates just after I graduated college. Ten years later, with Rae, it was when we were neighbors. Different cities, different decades, same joy. When Rae had to move out of her apartment across the street—she was adamant about staying on the same block—we became neighbors on the same side of the street separated by one house in between us. Few things have brought me as much comfort and happiness as being constantly immersed in the feeling of closeness and belonging that I got from living in such close proximity to dear friends. No matter how many times we hung out, it never got old. I was always excited to see each of them. Every interaction we shared cemented the bonds of our friendship.

Memories of those times float back to me in bits and pieces like scenes remembered from a favorite movie. There was the summer heat wave when it was too hot to sit inside and too hot to cook, so Rae and I grabbed whatever cold produce we had and threw together a fruit and veggie salad that we realized had every color of the rainbow in it. Or the time when Balthazar told me that he secretly liked Britney Spears, so I bought a copy of her fan magazine from the grocery store and plastered the pictures all over the door to his bedroom. Or the time when several days of snow shut down the city on Rae's birthday so we trudged with frozen toes to the neighborhood dive bar because it was the only place open and we had celebrating to do. Or the time when Balthazar tried to impress me by making blackened tofu but didn't realize that blackening seasoning is different from pure cayenne powder and that the two are not interchangeable.

There were many factors that made my friendships with Balthazar and Rae blossom. One factor that's often the least acknowledged is our addresses. In each case, the closeness we developed was only possible because we lived where we did. We stayed put for a long time and gave each other a lot of attention while we were there. My friendship with Balthazar had the additional benefit of developing inside a house that had no TV, smartphones, or internet. (Well, it was 52k dialup that was about as bad as not having any internet at all. We almost never used it.) When we weren't at work, we were often home and deeply present with each other. We talked for hours. We went for walks. We read books. We worked on art projects. We competed with each other in the kitchen. We spent our time the way people do now when they plunk down big money to go on digital detox retreats at idyllic cabins in the woods. Except it was our regular life. And we stayed put long enough to create friendships that will live on, no matter what our new addresses are.

The funny thing is, establishing each of these deep friendships didn't take a very long time. Balthazar and I only lived together for about two and a half years. After that, I moved across the country. Rae and I were neighbors for about the same amount of time. I've lived far away from each of them for much longer than that now. It's been fifteen years since I moved away from Balthazar, and seven since I moved away from Rae.

Building friendships that last doesn't necessarily take a long time. Wherever you are, settle in. Invest in the people who are right there with you. Ask your neighbors to come over for dinner or to go on neighborhood walks. Treat whatever is happening in real time like it's a million times more interesting than whatever is happening online. Make friends like this is the last place you'll ever live. If you're lucky, you'll end up with friends who stick around no matter where you go.

FITTING FRIENDSHIP INTO YOUR BUSY LIFE

One of the biggest complaints that comes up when people talk about friendship during adulthood is that "everyone's so busy all the time!" Countless memes about how hard it is to align our schedules and make plans to see friends fill up our Instagram and Twitter feeds. And yeah, it's true. Our full-time working years are likely to be the busiest in our lives since they overlap with our child-rearing years, our grad school years, our professional-achievement years and our being-in-a-grown-up-relationship years. This leads a lot of people to suffer from the delusion that they're too busy for friends. Let's be honest with ourselves. Maybe the reason we're "so busy" is because these are also our Netflix-bingeing years and our endless-scrolling-through-social-media years.

A busy life looks good on paper but it's often a pain in the ass in reality, and it is certainly not a vaccine against loneliness. Our collective agreement to accept lives defined by Generalized Busyness Disorder,[1] as if it's the only way or the best way to live, is a mistake that costs us in more ways than one. Research shows that the stress triggered by being overly busy can lead to fatigue, headaches, sleep problems, hyperemotionality, anxiety, and more.[2] Busyness can also be fatal to one of the things that's a salve for it: friendship. The good news is, we can change the rate of busyness in our lives if we want to. And when we can't change it, we can at least change the way we approach it, think about it, and deal with it.

In this chapter, we'll take a look at ways to get more free time while keeping your employment intact, and peek into the secrets of a spacious life. We'll explore ways to add more spaciousness to your life, and how to multiply the value of your friendships with the power of presence once you do.

Get (un) busy

A few years ago I attended a meetup called Oakland Neighbor's Table. Each month, a different person on the organizing committee would hold a lunch in their kitchen or living room, and lead a conversation on a specific topic by providing a few guiding questions to get things going. The day I attended, seven or eight of us munched on hastily assembled turkey and cheese sandwiches in a sunny, cozy apartment near Lake Merritt. The topic was busyness.

Throughout the conversation we kvetched about how busyness kept us from seeing other people as much as we'd like, and from doing things we wanted to do more of. We talked about the subtle social pressure to stay busy because busy people look productive and desirable. We also talked about strategies to avoid being so busy and ways to reclaim more balance in our lives. It was a lively conversation punctuated by people's confessions, regrets, and wishes for a more balanced life.

Sadly, a short while later the meetup disbanded. Maybe everyone got too busy. The Bay Area has a higher concentration of busy people than anywhere else I've lived. From the startup hopefuls and the steadfast political activists, to the self-improvement junkies and the constant flow of people moving in and out of the region, people are always on the go. What better place to tackle the job of learning how to be less busy? When I first started meditating I used to think that the best place to practice would be in the center of a crowded shopping mall on Black Friday—if you

can find nirvana there, you can find it anywhere. I feel the same way about trying to get unbusy in bustling big cities. Don't blame your environment. Defy it.

If you scoffed when you read that it takes 200 hours to make a new friend, because finding that kind of time seems impossible, then I am especially talking to you. It might seem like you're far too busy to fit friendship into your life. Are you though? We all wake up every day with the same number of hours on the clock. Some people fill every spare second with activities, meetings, and errands to run to, yet some people have time to read a book, take a nap, or practice the guitar. Too often we prioritize activities that allow us to report that we're keeping busy, and we jettison and play-down the ones that make us sound idle. A young man I interviewed in Berkeley said, "We have to let ourselves be free of the notion that we're supposed to be busy all the time. Even when we're not busy, we default to acting and behaving like we're supposed to be busy. We build walls around ourselves with busyness."[1]

Your calendar is not going to open itself up on its own, so if you're going to hurry at anything, hurry up and do less. Want to live a life that feels more free? The way to feel free is to act like you already are.

Take It Easy

Does it ever feel like life is a giant to-do list of things to check off, rather than an unfolding tapestry of experiences? If so, practice your capacity to surrender to spontaneity.

A report by *The Washington Post* found that people were happier when they didn't assign their free time activities to a specific time slot in their calendar, opting instead to do them spontaneously or during a nonspecific time frame. In their study, even something fun like getting ice cream with a friend was reported as more enjoyable when it wasn't assigned to an exact day and time in advance. Their findings showed that things that are supposed to be fun (e.g. writing a letter to a friend, practicing a creative hobby, having sex) feel less fun when they're scheduled. Rough scheduling, as opposed to strict scheduling, resulted in greater happiness and satisfaction for the participants in the study.[2] If you schedule things flexibly, you often approach them with more ease and you enjoy them more, too. Try it in the next couple of weeks and see how it feels.

TAKE CONTROL OF YOUR TIME

Let's say you've taken the admirable step of deciding that you're ready for a more fulfilling friendship experience and you're willing to do something to make it happen. Great first step. So you look at your life and huh, that's interesting…it looks like you're too busy for friends. Really? Do you lack the time—or do you lack the dedication? Have you considered that when you decided you were ready to "do something" to have better friendships, that this might actually mean "doing less things"? If your busyness doesn't spark joy, as the saying goes, then it's time to ditch it. If your busyness does spark joy, then ask your friends to join you on more of your busy-making activities.

Time Use Assessment

Let's get a handle on things. Get a pen and a piece of paper. Draw a line down the middle from top to bottom. On the left side, make a list of the distractions, time-sucks, and attention-grabbers that continually succeed at getting you to squander your precious time. Then write down approximately how many minutes per day, week, or month that you currently give to them.

Here's an example:

Social media

1 hour per day (30 mins. while commuting, 30 mins. at home)

x 5 days a week = 5 hours per week

x 52 weeks per year = 260 hours per year (10.8 days per year)

That's at least ten solid 24-hour days per year just scrolling, clicking 'like,' and blabbing into the bottomless pit of the internet. Bonus point: Review your daily log of screen time; most phones will provide you with this sobering data free of charge though you may have to dig in the settings to find it.

Watching Netflix

2 hours per day

x 4 days a week = 8 hours per week

x 52 weeks per year = 416 hours per year, or 17.3 solid 24-hour days per year. This is a modest estimate. According to a Nielsen report, the average American watches 5 hours of TV every day, which works out to 1,825 hours or 77 days per year.[1] Damn.

After you make a list of your time-sucks, make a list on the right side of all the things you'd rather be devoting your time to. Give this list a fun name. It can include hopes, aspirations, and curiosities. Be imaginative and lavish as you list out the things you'd like to do in your life and in your friendships. When your list

is at least one page long, read it over. Everything you put on this list is what you're trading away every time you give your minutes and hours to the list of time-wasters. Hopefully, seeing the way your lost time stacks up, you'll start to see where you can compile that "200 hours it takes to make a friend" after all.

Next, grab a red pen and draw some big juicy arrows from the time-wasters you're ready to relinquish or reduce to the things on the life-giving list that you want to replace them with. Consider, as technology ethicist James Williams says, whether your distractions are "keeping you from living the life you want to live."[2] What are the things you want to do that will give back to you in fulfillment, connection, happiness, and joy? Prioritize those things. Who are the people who make you smile, who you love talking to, and who you love being around? Prioritize having moments of connection and time with those people. How hard would it be to replace some of your distractions with intentional actions that will cultivate the friendship and meaningful connections you want?

Here are some easy examples of things you can do with all the time you've gained back:

Send a thoughtful note to a friend(s)
20 minutes

Go for a walk with a neighbor that you want to be friends with
30 minutes

Call a friend on the phone
2 hours

What else would you do if your biggest goal for the year was cultivating one or two deeper friendships, and you now realize that you have more than enough time to make it happen?

MAKE ROOM FOR
SPACIOUSNESS

If busyness is the state of having a life choked off by an endlessly full calendar, then its dreamy opposite is spaciousness. Mmmm, spaciousness. Even saying it is soothing. Go ahead, say it out loud, and feel your jaw suddenly unclench. Spaciousness. It sits side by side with the openness we talked about in the Seeds of Connection chapter. One of my favorite stories about openness and spaciousness comes from my friend Jabu.[1]

When she moved from Oakland, California, to Santa Fe, New Mexico, Jabu said that one of the most striking differences was the level of openness that people in Santa Fe showed towards her, and how a sense of spacious flexibility permeated many interactions. After just one conversation, people would invite her to come over to their house for dinner, or they'd ask her to hang out on the weekend and actually follow up. They didn't want anything from her, except to spend time together. Their calendars were open in a way that peoples' calendars in the Bay Area were generally not. Their minds were open in a different way too. In the Bay Area, invitations like the ones she was receiving might not come your way after knowing someone for months or even years.

People living in cities marked by high achievement like New York, San Francisco, and Los Angeles have told me that it feels like their city is characterized by constant striving. A lot of social interactions have an underlying energy of competition and value extraction. There's a thinly veiled aura of "What can you do for me? How can I prove myself to you? How will knowing you serve my goals? What are you going to ask from me?" It's all very transactional.

In contrast, Jabu explained that the people she met in Santa Fe were interested in getting to know people based on their curiosity about them, not based on the value they can extract from them. Spaciousness and openness permeated their calendars and interactions. People there treated the word "connection" like the outcome of authentic relating, not as a noun used to refer to a person in your professional network. One day, she described a recent evening she had spent with a rather motley crew of new friends to me over the phone. Her hairdresser friend had invited her to come over to his house, where her trim and dye would take place. During the beautification session, they were joined by the hairdresser's husband who served as the town's police chief and their eighty-year-old widow friend who was mixing up some mean cocktails for all of them. The blend of ages, interests, life stages, and jobs in that vignette were so dramatically different from groupings that Jabu was used to observing in the Bay Area where people tended to socialize in more homogenous groupings based on age and industry; the biggest divide was always between those who work in technology and those who don't. In Jabu's story, she and her three new friends all had free time at the same time, and that was enough to make them all worthy of sharing it together.

Just Sit There

One way to add more openness and spaciousness to your life is to embrace the Dutch concept of Niksen. In an article in *Time* magazine, Caroline Hamming, managing director of CSR Centrum, a coaching center in the Netherlands that helps people recover from burnout and stress, defined Niksen as "to do nothing, to be idle or doing something without any use."[2] You don't have a goal, a purpose, or any instructions. You just let yourself be and let your mind wander. If this sounds terribly uncomfortable, she says you can start with five or ten minutes. Work your way up to one whole evening a week. For more inspiration on cultivating your ability to be fully present, check out the book *How to Do Nothing* by Jenny O'Dell.

ReCONTEXTUALIZe BUSY

My friend Jed in London has adopted a novel approach to keep himself accountable for busyness in his calendar. He's been practicing eliminating the phrase "I'm busy" from his vocabulary and avoids using that generic phrase as an excuse or answer for anything. Whenever someone asks him how he's been, he doesn't say, "I've been really busy." He tells them what he's actually been spending his time on. If someone asks him to do something at a time when he has other plans, he's specific when he declines. If he would rather exercise than go to a movie, he won't just say, "I'm busy that day"—he'll say, "I've been trying to stick to my fitness goals, and I have a commitment with myself to exercise at that time."[1] He said that this practice makes him check himself to make sure he's not just copping out by using a vague reply that modern society takes as an acceptable or even admirable answer. An additional bonus is that by being specific, he lets the other person in on more details of his life. It often sparks a conversation, or leads him to feel closer to the other person.

Whenever I catch myself defaulting to the habit of thinking "I'm so busy" or that my schedule is too busy, I try to remind myself that life is just an ongoing process of things happening. If I wasn't doing the things that happen to already be booked into

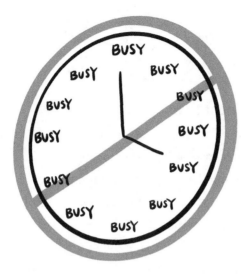

the hours of my life, I'd be doing different things. Every single minute of the day is filled to the brim with that particular slice of life happening. We can choose to fill a single minute with whatever we want: running for the bus, giving a long hug to a friend, shaking our booties to Daft Punk, writing a postcard to a friend, staring at our phones, watching the birds on the telephone line, or noticing our breath entering and exiting our lungs. If we choose to spend twelve hours at a meditation retreat or at twelve different locations spread all over town, those twelve hours will be filled to the same capacity: twelve hours in total. So, in a way, busyness is less about the fullness of our days, and more so about the way we feel as those days pass by. Busyness is a choice and a mindset. It's an attitude that many of us are addicted to identifying with. And it's a habitual way of thinking that we are capable of setting aside when we're ready to feel our days, and fill our days, with whatever thoughts and actions we decide would be more beautiful and fulfilling.

A Week Without Time

For one full week, cover all the clocks in your house. Of course, set an alarm to wake you up, and any others that you need for specific reminders. But aside from that, ignore the clock. The idea here is to let yourself be more in tune with what you're drawn to do in the moment based on what feels right to you, instead of when the clock says you're supposed to. Eat when you want, and go to bed when you feel tired. Listen to yourself. Free yourself from the feelings of urgency and pressure that can come from paying attention to time passing.

Do a 30-Day Busyness Detox

For one month, say "no" to as many scheduled invitations or obligations as you can. Recruit an acquaintance, friend, or coworker to join you in the pursuit of gloriously unscheduled free time.

Then, save four to eight hours of "Me Time" in your calendar every week. It doesn't matter if you take it as an hour at dawn and thirty minutes before bed, or as a few solid two-hour blocks. Don't assign specific tasks to these time blocks, just hold them and then fill them in the moment with what you want to be doing right then.

Delete all social media apps from your phone and log out of them in your browser. Only read on paper: books, magazines, newspapers. No reading online; it's too easy to get pulled into things that feel like work or to lose three hours falling down a rabbit hole. Whatever your current amount of TV and movie consumption is, cut it in half. Don't bloat your calendar. See some unscheduled blocks? Leave them there so you have the freedom to be spontaneous.

When you have to do errands, see how you can adjust them to make them feel 20 percent more like leisure time. One of my favorite ways to do this is to go grocery shopping at an odd hour when the store is super empty and listen to a favorite podcast or a new album as I leisurely stroll the empty aisles.

If you feel bored sometimes, allow yourself to notice what boredom feels like. Look around you and notice the things you have been ignoring while the attention economy has dominated your senses. For these thirty days of your life, let yourself feel freer than you've ever felt before.

Want more ideas? Check out:

A Helpful Guide to Becoming Unbusy:
www.becomingminimalist.com/un-busy/

Blog: Becoming Unbusy
www.becomingunbusy.com/

The Bored and Brilliant Challenge
www.wnyc.org/series/bored-and-brilliant

DOUBLE DOWN ON SHOWING UP

As an introvert who loves to spend my free time alone working on projects, thinking, reflecting, and creating, I can be satisfied in solitude for a long time. I've found that these traits are well accepted on the West Coast, where a lot of people automatically assume that you have a side hustle and a passion project or two. When I realized I was having a hard time forming friendships and community here, I took it seriously and took steps to fix it. Now I have the opposite problem: I don't have enough time to see all my friends as often as I want to. I have to be careful about how many friendships I commit to because I don't want to get into a situation where I don't have the bandwidth to give each person the amount of time they deserve. How did I turn my situation around? I doubled down on showing up.

A basic but critical part of nurturing relationships is the act of following up and checking in with people. Because I know that being an absent-minded adult with a full life can make it too easy to forget to do this task regularly, I gave my brain some outside assistance. I scheduled repeating reminders in my phone to reach out to both my old friends and new friends. "Old friends" include anyone I've known more than two years. "New friends" include anyone I've met in the last one to two years.

MICRO-DOSING FRIENDSHIP CALENDAR

The "old friends" reminder includes five names; so does the "new friends" reminder (and I periodically refresh the set of names) Each week, one reminder pings me. This is a notification worth getting.

When I get the notification, I pick one or two people from the list and reach out. Sometimes I set up a time to connect 1:1, such as a meal, phone call, or walk. Sometimes I just let them know I'm thinking about them. I might drop a postcard in the mail or send them an article, photo, song, or podcast that I think they'd like. It might sound weird to have reminders to check in on my friends, but I swear it has done wonders for the continuity of my connection with friends near and far. Connection has become a supported habit.

After having lunch with one of my new friends recently, she thanked me for being so thoughtful and commented on how consistent I am in reaching out to her about getting together.

I told her about my method because I felt weird taking credit for it. What matters is the impact.

Now I'm seeing my friends more often in three months than I was previously seeing them in a year. With my friend Balthazar who lives on the opposite coast, we agreed that we'll talk every single weekend so that we can keep up our momentum. We stick to it, even when we have a lot going on in our lives and can only find five minutes to talk. The consistency of contact gives us a reliable sense of presence in each other's lives.

Cigna's oft-cited study about loneliness found that only around half of Americans have meaningful in-person social interactions—such as having an extended conversation or spending quality time with a friend or family member—on a daily basis.[1] It may sound nerdy, but you just might need to start booking Friend Time into your calendar and fiercely protecting those special blocks of time. A daily dose of connection will help the most, but like exercise, a couple times a week is better than none. Does every one of those blocks have to result in the deepest conversation of your life? Of course not. But if you're going to show up, really show up—emotionally as well as physically.

Get regular time with a friend who you can be yourself with. Make sure you don't only chit chat about the rain, the local sports team, or gossip about people you know in common. Talk about thoughts and feelings, and listen deeply while the other person shares about themselves, too. If something's been bothering you or keeping you awake at night, use this opportunity to get it off your chest. If you feel awkward bringing up something personal, check first that the other person is in the right headspace to really

COMPLAIN ABOUT
YOUR JOBS

TALK ABOUT HOW YOUR
LIFE IS GOING OVERALL

TALK ABOUT
THE WEATHER

SHARE DEEPEST
HOPES, FEARS,
SECRETS &
WISHES

TRUST-O-METER 5000

hear you: "Can I change the topic for a minute? I'd like to talk about something that's been on my mind, maybe get your perspective on it?"

Brené Brown's research on vulnerability has shown that taking action to be vulnerable with the other person first is key to deepening feelings of trust. You don't sit around waiting until the Trust-o-meter 5000 gives you a green light to be vulnerable. In *Daring Greatly*, Brown writes, "Vulnerability begets vulnerability; courage is contagious."[2] Be vulnerable first and see how that unlocks deeper levels of trust for you both.

You might be thinking, "Okay, that sounds nice, but I'm not that deep. I don't have anything important to talk about." That's fine. It doesn't mean you have to be lonely or bored by mind-numbing nonversations.[3] Make your Friend Time something that you can both enjoy doing together. Gardening, organizing, journaling, collaging, board games, ping pong, puzzles, card games, and video games can all facilitate bonding. The point is to share quality time with friends on a regular basis. All you have to do is make the time for it, and then show up.

Embrace the Telephone

If your life feels too busy for a bunch of in-person friend dates, embrace the ease, flexibility, and simplicity of the humble phone call. Digital devices have made it convenient to "talk" via short and instant text messages, but there's nothing like hearing someone's voice in a real time conversation for creating a sense of connection. If you want to be closer to a friend that you usually only text with, interact with on social media, or that it's hard to see face to face, ask if they're open to having phone calls. Even a short twenty minute chat can do wonders for fostering feelings of belonging and connection.

Friendship Staycation Weekend

Many interviewees described the fulfillment they get from spending a weekend with a dear friend who unfortunately now lives far away. As I was leaving one such weekend with my friend Balthazar on the east coast, he quipped, "This was like forty phonecalls combined." Why should we save such in-depth friendship immersions just for friends who live a plane ticket away? Have a forty-phonecall-weekend with an in-town friend, too. No, that doesn't mean literally making forty phone calls. It's an in-town "un-getaway" weekend that you spend at one of your houses. Think of it like a platonic grownup slumber party weekend. The friend who is coming over packs everything they'll need, just as if they were going on a trip to visit a friend in another state. Then, be together as if you are visiting from out of state. Sleep in the same place, eat your meals together, put your phone away, talk at the kitchen table, cook and clean up meals together. When you get bored, just sit there, or go for walks to explore your surroundings.

If you want this to be more exciting, use my friend Lila's strategy. As soon as she realizes how much she likes someone she wants to be closer friends with, she asks the new friend to go away on a weekend trip. They can each bring their partners or a couple other friends if they want. But she tries to get the other person to say yes to this itty bitty vacation together as soon as possible. She's not into camping so she'll find an Airbnb that everyone can chip in on together. "Preferably with a hot tub!" she laughs. It doesn't even have to be far away; the distance or location are not the point.

"Everyone's so busy that it's nearly impossible to find time to get close to a new friend and really build a strong connection. But in a weekend, you're together so much that you really can get a deeper connection going. You see each other when you wake up and you're all groggy. You see each other when you're hanging out in the hot tub, you make food together, you go for walks, you can do so much in a short amount of time. Then you have this cool memory together."[4]

Talk to two to three friends that you want to have a friendship staycation weekend with, and start scheming to make it happen.

BLENDING FRIENDSHIP
with
PARTNERSHIP & FAMILY

Like relocation, there's another life transition that often serves as a hurdle to making and maintaining friendships during adulthood. Despite its downsides for platonic friendship, this milestone generally tends to bring joy into people's lives: the arrival of a life partner and/or having kids.

According to a report by Oxford evolutionary anthropologist Robin Dunbar (of the famous Dunbar Number which states that humans can comfortably maintain a consistent and ongoing relationship with only 150 other people[1]), starting a new romantic relationship typically leads to the loss of two close friends.[2] This doesn't happen because of a direct fight or falling out, but because of the huge investment of time that a new romance requires. There's just not enough time for everyone. As a result, two people in the intimates/best friends circle get nudged out to the next ring of the social circle where less emotionally intimate friendships reside. Having children can cause a similar friendship attrition to occur because of the time required to care for babies and raise children—plus, the resulting exhaustion. As I discovered, it gets even more complicated than that.

In this chapter, we'll look at the most common way that romantic relationships (no matter how lovely) can squelch friendships. We'll touch on a strategy I call three-way balance that can help you keep your friendships and romantic partnerships in perfect harmony. Following that we'll look at friendships and family. Parents often face unique friendship challenges that those of us who are childless never have to consider. Consequently, this chapter devotes more time to exploring those specific hurdles and ways to handle them.

DUDE, WHERE'S MY FRIENDS?

Even people lucky enough to remain in the VIP best friends circle after their pal starts a new relationship might feel irritated at how it impacts their friendship dynamic. Levi, a music teacher in Seattle, spoke at length about this most common consequence of romantic relationship. "My problem isn't that my friends are moving away, it's that they're moving away from me compatibility-wise.[1] Friends are a huge priority in my life. I was close with a lot of friends in my twenties, but now we're in our thirties and I feel like I was a placeholder until they got a grown-up job, baby, marriage, or other status symbols that aren't goals for me," he said. "My goal for dating was never to disappear and have one person be my entire life." Levi has dealt with losing multiple friends when they found partners and subsequently vanished. Even if he's happy that his friends found love, being ditched is the pits.

Some of his partnered friends still text back, call, and show up to hang out, but they're so enveloped in their relationships that they hardly function as an individual person anymore. "A huge pet peeve of mine is when I ask a friend to hang out, and they respond with 'Yeah, *we'd* love to.'" He doesn't have anything against his friends' partners, but he wants to spend quality time with his friend as an individual human being—the one he has known and cared for since before their love interest came onto the scene. Once a friend has dissolved into their romantic relationship, it can feel like that person's gone, even if they're still sitting across from you at the dinner table.

When you're in a relationship yourself, there are other potential friendship challenges: seeing friends as a couple, seeing friends alone, not liking each other's friends or not being liked by your partner's friends. In the event of a breakup, there's the compounded issue of either losing mutual friends in the breakup, or realizing that you're extra lonely because you let your friendships fizzle out while you were coupled up. It doesn't have to be that way. What to do about it? Practice three-sided balance.

Three-sided Balance

Be intentional about using your time to connect with: mutual friends that you met as a couple, each partner's set of friends that you established before or outside the relationship, and last but not least, seeing individual friends by yourself. Getting together purposefully with each type of friend will help keep your relationship balanced and meet each person's friendship needs.

Spending time as a couple with mutual friends that you met as an existing couple can galvanize your relationship. It allows you to become known, and to express yourself, as a unit. The risk here is having your personal identity erased as you're absorbed into the singular unit of the relationship, as Levi vented about above. That's why this shouldn't be your only way of seeing friends.

Spending time as a couple with each partner's existing friends can deepen your perspective about your partner. You get to learn what traits they value in other people, and their friends can give you insight into how your partner has grown over time. The risk here is that there's an inherent imbalance anytime you're hanging out with only one partner's friend group—that partner obviously has more rapport with their own friends, and so the partner whose friends aren't present may feel alienated or less emotionally fulfilled.

Spending time apart hanging out with your friends solo gives you the chance to be known as an individual. And let's face it, sometimes you'll need a confidential place to vent about your partner or to ask for relationship advice. The risk here is that if you only see your friends separately, you miss out on building the trust that comes from letting your partner and friends get to know each other. Taken to extremes, this distancing can lead to suspicion, jealousy, or resentment.

Maintaining a healthy relationship takes a significant investment of time, but remember that your friendships are a type of relationship too. Your friendships deserve to be nurtured, and you deserve to be nurtured by them, too.

LONELY PARENT

An involuntary friendship dissolution often happens when friends have babies and begin raising kids. The extra time needed for parenting is usually pulled from the "Time with Friends" bucket. While cutting out friends can support your ability to give attention to your partner or kids in the short term, it simultaneously weakens your support network. This impact hits single parents the hardest, who have some of the highest rates of loneliness in America.[1] Still, coupled parents can also suffer from disorienting bouts of loneliness. "After I became a dad, my social life atrophied practically overnight," writes Jason McBride in *Today's Parent.*[2]

I'm not a parent, and I have no aspirations to become one, so I have genuinely tried to understand the challenges parents face around friendship. From what I can tell, parents have it especially hard because they face the same challenges that single people do, but they have additional challenges that only come with being a parent.

One cause of the loneliness that parents face stems from the challenge of a changing identity, or the loss thereof. Becoming a parent can easily overwrite one's sense of self. Mia, a writer for *HuffPost* faced this challenge herself when she was on the verge of becoming a mother. "When we think about identity theft, we think about an impostor posing as another person. Yet in motherhood, we are the imposters in our own lives."[3] Amy, a mother of two middle schoolers living outside Atlanta, also finds it frustrating when her role as a mother overshadows the rest of her identity. "I'm forty-one now and essentially a fulltime mom when I'm not working on my business," she told me.[4] When she meets new people, they can't see the adventurous, playful, energetic dancer she used to be, who could dance all night and also practiced Capoeira in her spare time. "In my twenties I used to be the kind of person who would work a double, go dancing 'til 3 a.m., sleep a few hours, then wake up and work another double. Of course my life isn't like that anymore, but I'm not just some mom who's taking her kids to soccer practice." The lives we've lived make us who we are. Our past journeys don't get erased just because they're not visible from where we stand today, but parenthood can make it feel that way.

Sometimes the thing you don't feel like you have time for—like friends—is exactly what you need to help you feel like yourself again. For Jordan, a writer in Silicon Valley, venting to other women who also saw their professional identities as writers, lawyers, and teachers usurped by the messy, overwhelming world of new motherhood. Finding support meant being vulnerable and honest about her challenges. "When we lay our struggles and our worst selves bare, we help others feel less alone,"[5] she wrote in the online magazine *Quartz*. Mia also realized that maintaining her own identity in motherhood would mean making an extra effort to not let go of the activities, goals, and modes of self-expression that loved pre-motherhood.

For Julie, a mother in Los Angeles, giving extra attention to her social life helped her keep her identity balanced. "Our friends help remind us who we are outside of parenting,"[6] she says. She purposely tries to spend time with friends with whom she can talk about anything *except* kids. She also recommends not over-scheduling your kids' activities, so that you don't end up over scheduling yourself as their chauffeur. That leaves you more time to plan activities for yourself, or to just give yourself some much-needed downtime.

If you're in the market for new parent friends, one excellent approach for making parent friends is to ignore the "parent" part of that goal, and just focus on making *friends*. Author Rebecca Lang described on *Motherly* how she had a much better time connecting with potential friends when she focused more on what the other person was like as a regular person, not as a parent whose skills and choices she might find herself judging if they were different from her own. She tries to get into a conversation focused on something beyond naps, schools and sleep schedules, opting instead to take advantage of the fact that a conversation with another adult is an opportunity to have an interaction that isn't about kids.[7] Remember that you're a full person beyond your role as a partner or parent. See your potential new friends—or old friends—the same way too.

Blast from the Past

It's a lot easier to catch someone up on what's happened in your life since the last time you talked (e.g. an old friend) than it is to catch someone up on what's happened in the entirety of your life (e.g. a new friend). Ten minutes spent with someone who knows your context and history can be more fulfilling than spending an hour talking with someone who doesn't know you at all. Plus, these are likely to be people who knew you before you became a parent, so they have a more full view of you as a person.

Even if you haven't stayed in touch consistently, there's success to be had in reaching out to someone you haven't talked to since college or high school. I've heard multiple accounts of people picking up right where they left off, even if years or decades had passed in between. Don't underestimate the power of reconnecting with an old friend, in person or on the phone.

Nurture Existing Friendships

If you're about to or have recently become a new parent, assure your friends that you want to remain close even after the baby arrives. One of my best friends, Annie, and I recently faced this milestone together. In conversations before her first baby, Audre, was born and during the next couple months, we checked in with each other often to reaffirm our commitment to our friendship. In face-to-face conversations, phone calls, and texts, we joyfully (and sometimes tearfully) talked about what we feared might change in our friendship, as well as what we cherished about each other and wanted to hold onto. After Audre was born, I took extra steps to show my dedication by bringing food and offering to help with any baby or household needs, and Annie took extra steps to keep in touch and make time for face-to-face hangouts at both of our houses. At one of our recent hangouts, I told Annie how much it meant to me that she's continued to prioritize our friendship despite the demands of motherhood. "This baby is part of the team,"[8] Annie laughed. "You and I are definitely gonna keep seeing each other, and Audre's coming along for the ride!" With dedication, commitment, and clear expressions of intent, you too can ensure that your family and your friendships both continue to thrive.

BFFs + 1

PARENT TOWN

When proactively looking for new friends, unusual road-blocks that kid-free people never have to think about can crop up for parents. Gabrielle, a mother of a preschooler in Brooklyn, summed up one challenge she's had booking play dates. "We can't get the parents across the street from us to hang out with us even though our kids are the same age. Why? Because our side of the street is assigned to one public school and their side of the street is assigned to another public school. They'd rather spend time with families whose kids go to the same school as their kids. Even though we live right across the street! It's just more convenient for them to socialize and schedule things with the families that they'll naturally keep seeing at the same school functions,"[1] she said. This blew my mind. That's like a person refusing to make friends with a neighbor because they don't work in the same office building. What could be more convenient than having friends in the house directly across from you?

Gabrielle is on the right track, though, by trying to make friends in such close proximity. Public school assignments notwithstanding, having friends within walking distance is one of the best things you can do to provide emotional support and a social safety net for you and your kids. Gabrielle kept searching and was eventually able to connect with another family who just moved to her block and were looking for new friends. If you run into a fluke like Gabrielle's, laugh it off and keep trying. You'll find your people.

Go Hyperlocal

The population-weighted density of the average US metro area is approximately 6,000 people per square mile, and it's even as high as about 12,000 people per square mile in larger cities like San Francisco and Los Angeles.[2] That's a lot of potential matches for new friends and walkable play dates! Try to make friends with families who live within walking distance from you, whether you consider walking distance to be one block or ten. This will give your kids the psychological benefit of having friends nearby, and it will be less stressful to make play dates that don't involve driving and parking.

Keeping Everyone Happy

Another complicating factor is the prospect of hanging out as a whole family. Since free time is scarce, full family hangouts are more efficient. A mother of three in San Francisco described how hard it is to arrange hangouts with another family when there are five boxes of satisfaction to check: one for her, one for her husband, and one for each of their three kids.[1] It's not enough for her to like the one other parent she wants to hang out with. Their partners need to like each other, and both families' sets of kids need to like each other too. If one piece of that multipronged matchmaking experiment fails, it's a lot harder to get everyone to hang out again.

TRY TO LIKE THESE OTHER KIDS BECAUSE
I REALLY WANNA BE FRIENDS WITH
THEIR MOM, OK?

Bigger Invites

Instead of putting so much pressure on having a match between everyone in your family and one other family, let your partner and kids invite people to a multi-family hangout. That way, each person will have at least one other friend present who they connect with. Don't forget to invite your single and childfree friends, too. Just because they don't have partners or kids doesn't meant they don't want to see you; they're also a perfect fit if you're looking for someone to have conversation with about non-parenting-related topics. If your house is too small for a big gathering, pick somewhere free and flexible like a local park.

OUTSIDE LOOKING IN

Finding another parent who you want to be friends with in the first place can also be daunting. Gabrielle from Brooklyn talked about the tongue-in-cheek advice that she got when she looked into enrolling her daughter in kindergarten.[1] Another mother half-jokingly told her to snatch up her parent friends during the kindergarten year because after first grade, she'd be screwed. All the prospective parent-kid friendship units would be buddied up by then and no longer open to newcomers. This was echoed by Ruth, a mom in Seattle, who felt the brunt of showing up too late to the party. She described how hard it was for her to be accepted by the other moms, even though her family moved to the neighborhood eight years ago. "My youngest is two years into her new school and so far I've only made connections with two other families,"[2] she said. "I joined the local parent Facebook group, I help in the community, but no matter what, people are still reluctant to include you in things, even conversations."

As if all that wasn't enough, the cherry on top is the added pressure of competition, flexed in person as well as online. One mother in Oakland described how Helicopter parents have now morphed into Bulldozer/Snowplow Parents who dedicate their entire life to removing every obstruction from their kid's path. This overprotective habit results in more fragile children and it can lead to parents treating other families as obstacles and opponents, rather than as sources of camaraderie and connection.[3]

Ruth lamented, "People leave people out on purpose. I've had moms not pass on info about school matters just to have their kids at an advantage." In her world, social media exacerbates the atmosphere of competition and one-upmanship. "Friendships are so fake in this day and age. Most of the parents in my community are self-consumed and social-media-crazy. One particular mom posts so much crap about her kid on social media, you'd think she's trying to get them voted for prom already." Ruth is frustrated by the pressure to constantly project a perfect image online, and she hates the way social media habits can inhibit down-to-earth interactions.

Making friends has been a hard road, but she makes progress in tiny steps. She starts by asking other moms out for coffee. If they click, she invites them to bring their family over to her house so their spouses and kids can meet. She's had the best luck with moms who can focus on genuine conversation and aren't trying to post pictures of their hangout on social media every time they see each other.

Cut to the Chase

Ask other parents what their experience of friendship has been like since they became parents. Talk about your challenges and the things you wish for. When you're short on time, cranking up your level of vulnerability and opening up about your own struggles can go a long way towards building closeness.

Bonus: If you really knew me

When making friends with new parent, move beyond the small talk about feeding schedules and sleeping habits. Set aside a specific block of time for the purpose of getting to know each other better. Set a timer for five or ten minutes, then take turns completing this sentence out loud:

"If you really knew me, you would know that _____."

Go back and forth, sharing anything that is true for you that a person couldn't know by looking at you. You can choose to share small things or big things. The level of self-disclosure is up to you based on your comfort level, but remember the point of the activity is to get to know each other on a deeper level.[4] Afterwards, talk about how it felt to share this activity. What things did you have in common? What things surprised you? What conversations and ideas were sparked by learning more about each other?

Enjoy the Moment

See what it feels like to spend time with other parents and kids without posting any pictures or updates about it on social media. If you want to keep a memory of the day, work on a collage or a drawing (this book is proof that stick figures count) to capture a special moment from your time together. Or, after you go home, take one minute and send your friend a note to let them know how much it meant to you to spend time together.

REMEMBER TO BREATHE

My dear friend Sarah, a mother of three, wrote this poem when her kids were still young and just starting school. It captures many parts of her new motherhood experience: care, concern, platonic longing, and hope. I think it says more than I could ever say about parenthood and friendship, from a place of knowing that I will never know. (Reprinted with her permission.)[1]

Warp and Weft
by Sarah Dunning Park

Somewhere along the line,
your friends dispersed
like seeds scooped from a sack,
a few slipping through fingers
and back in the bag with you—
the rest flying out, pitched to far cities,
to root down in places
other than here.

Here, you inch forward
in a line of cars, wondering if
the other mothers dropping off kids
are like you, or if they would like you—
and pondering the irony

that you are alike at least in this:
each of you has narrowed
the scope of your focus
to encompass only
the most pressing needs
of your family.

But you remember
when you'd woven your living
in with the weft of your friends'—
not planning social events
in the cracks of packed schedules,
but pooling your leftovers
to share improvised meals.

Most days, now, you improvise alone—
if you don't mind defining *alone*
as shadowed by a chattering child—
and later you commune with friends
through a cold screen.

You spend your time observing
your child's likes and dislikes
and which scraps of thought
she chooses to voice;
you try to see these
as seeds of her adult self—
like fiddlehead ferns

with their Fibonacci spirals,
slowly unfurling.

You can picture, down the line,
the fully opened fronds
and how they'll form a crown of green—
this is how you remind yourself
that in time, and with luck,
she'll become your dear friend.

But it's not enough, or it's too much
that you've concentrated on one spot,
like a magnifying glass
clutched in patient suspension,
intensifying the rays of the sun
to the point of combustion.

You must widen your gaze.
Recall the critical importance
of dropping your shoulders
and allowing your chest to rise,
to draw open your lungs,
to permit the intake
of a full breath. And then—
remember your need
for friends to stand beside you
and breathe too.

THINGS THAT ARE SCARY ABOUT TRYING TO MAKE NEW FRIENDS

- ASKING THEM TO HANG OUT WITHOUT SEEMING LIKE A STALKER.

- THINKING ABOUT THINGS TO TALK ABOUT IN THE MOMENT.

- NERVOUS LAUGHTER...

- HAVE TO PAY ATTENTION. CAN'T CHECK PHONE!

- 3-4 SECONDS OF SILENCE MIGHT HAPPEN. MAYBE MORE!?

- WHAT IF THEY THINK I'M TRYING TO DATE/FLIRT WITH THEM?! I ONLY WANT TO BE FRIENDS...

- WHAT IF THEY DON'T WANT TO BE FRIENDS WITH ME, OR WE'RE NOT COMPATIBLE?

- WHAT IF THEY REALLY WANT TO BE FRIENDS WITH ME, BUT I END UP NOT REALLY LIKING THEM AFTER ALL? OR VICE VERSA?

- IF THIS DOESN'T WORK OUT, I HAVE TO START THE WHOLE PROCESS OVER AGAIN WITH SOMEONE ELSE...

GETTING BETTER
at
GETTING CLOSER

The last challenge to overcome on our journey towards friendship fulfillment is the closest to home. It's also the thing we have the most control over: ourselves. Our ability to bond with others and maintain durable friendships is inversely proportional to the walls that we build around our hearts.

There are many kinds of walls. Some walls are made of smartphones and apps. Some walls are made of busyness and schedules that prevent us from sitting still long enough to get close. Some walls are made of frightened hearts and the lips they keep unnecessarily zipped in moments of soft and safe intimacy. Some walls are made of the incomplete maps we carry for navigating unfamiliar emotional territory. Some walls are made of the one-sided imitation friendships we maintain with the celebrities and entertainers we follow and listen to daily, who don't even know that we exist. The toughest walls are made of our own stubborn refusal to be vulnerable and brave in our pursuit of fulfilling friendships.

It's critical that we approach our endeavors to rehabilitate our withering capacity for intimacy with gusto. We must focus and be intentional in our pursuit. To take back our attention and our time, and to repurpose it for building the connections we deserve, we'll have to summon up as much courage and ingenuity as we can. If we succeed at this, we'll have access to the most precious thing that money can't buy: each other.

In this chapter, we'll examine how device-mediated lives interrupt our instincts and ability to connect in real life. We'll explore how entertaining substitutions for friendship can be dangerously palliative in how they subtly encourage us to stop trying to cultivate the real thing. We'll also review a collection of imaginative, audacious, and humble ways that people are embracing vulnerability in the pursuit of cultivating better friendships in their lives.

ANTISOCIAL MEDIA

Back when I was a habitual Facebook user, there was this thing that would happen that always perplexed me. I'd meet someone I wanted to be friends with, and I'd add them on Facebook. We'd quickly adopt the habit of interacting with each other's posts and this would become our default way of "talking." The norm of interacting online would usurp our budding IRL friendship. We'd "like" each other's posts instead of having longer conversations in person, going for walks, sharing meals, and doing other friend-ship-building activities. On a few occasions, this even happened when our houses were close enough to easily hang out face to face. We said we wanted to be friends, but then, instead of hanging out, we'd observe snippets of each other's lives online.

My wariness of Facebook grew when I noticed another phenomenon that other friends said they experienced too. It started to seem like sharing our life updates on social media had the unfortunate side effect of atrophying our existing friends' curiosity. People quit calling to hear how life was going because social media allowed them to feel like they already knew. The human brain is adept at creating simple stories and filling in the gaps. Snippets on social media make that easy. When you see "person standing in front of Eiffel Tower" or "smiling people in front of the ocean" or "latte art and a croissant in front of a window," you think you know what's going on, but maybe you don't. Social media platforms want you to share what you've been up to, but only on a surface level. They encourage us to skim the

news about the world and about our friends' lives. But real friendship isn't about skimming.

My former coworker Denise once relayed a story to me
about her frustration with the shift in her social circle away from
curiosity and towards shallow followership.[1] At the grocery store
she'd run into a friend who she used to hang out with. Her friend
cheerily mentioned seeing a picture from Denise's recent vacation
on Facebook. After a one-minute conversation, they parted
ways. It left Denise feeling strangely exposed and invisible at the
same time. She wondered if she hadn't posted about her trip
on Facebook, and had instead been able to tell her friend about
it spontaneously in real life, would the chance interaction have
catalyzed more togetherness?

REALITY:

ALSO REALITY:

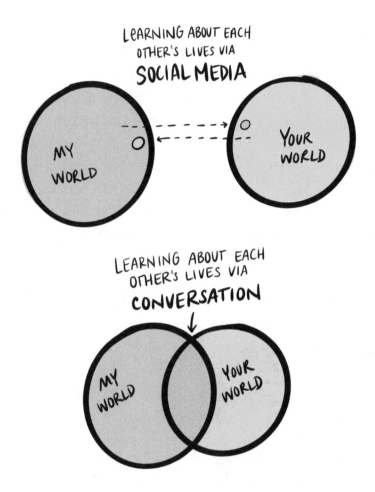

Social media posts give their viewers the illusion of having shared a meaningful interaction with the person who posted it. Meanwhile, the person who posted it may not even know that the viewer saw it. Does the person who shares on social media need each individual person in their audience, or do they just need *an* audience? When we share, what exactly is shared? Certainly not a moment of meaningful connection. If I execute the one-way transfer of a tiny piece of my personal data into your awareness, you might know more about me or my life, but does that mean we've grown closer to each other? I don't think so.

Following our friends' lives on social media subjects us to a cognitive bias where the spectator starts thinking that they're closer than they really are to someone whose information they're consuming. "Follow anyone long enough and you feel like you are a part of their life," says Madison Means in the online magazine *Odyssey*. That is the conclusion she came to after writing about how Instagram led her to feel like she was really friends with one of her favorite country music stars, Thomas Rhett and his wife, Lauren.[2]

In the 1950s, psychologists Richard Wohl and Donald Horton gave this phenomenon a name: parasocial interaction.[3] It's what

you call the imaginary psychological relationship that fans think they have with celebrities. Wohl and Horton's theory was based on their observations of viewers and listeners of mass media personalities via radio and TV. Nowadays when most people have hundreds, if not thousands, of followers on social media, we're all tiny celebrities in our own microscopic universes. Our followers, like Denise's friend in the grocery store, think they really know us

**" I THINK MY FRIENDS LIKE MY CONTENT
MORE THAN THEY LIKE ME."**

and know how we are based on the snippets we publish to our
Facebook, Instagram, and Twitter feeds.

Relationships mediated by digital devices "give us the illusion
of companionship without the demands of friendship,"[4] writes
Sherry Turkle, a PhD and professor of the Social Studies of
Science and Technology at MIT, in her book *Alone Together: Why
We Expect More from Technology and Less from Each Other.* Denise's
friend felt like she did her part by consuming that tidbit of data
about Denise's life. But she didn't show up for Denise the way a
real friend would—with genuine curiosity and interested attention.

One woman I interviewed in San Francisco described the
disorientation she felt after posting about the death of a family
member on social media. Her friends commented and "liked" the
post, but didn't follow up with her in real life to see how she was
doing or to offer support in a deeper way. "How am I supposed to

interpret their lack of response? Especially when I know for sure that they saw it on my Instagram Story?"[5] she lamented.

If we think that sharing the abridged version of our lives on social media is snuffing out our budding friendships or curtailing the inquisitiveness of our existing friends, we have the power to break that pattern. We can reject the notion that sharing updates about our lives should primarily happen on platforms owned by companies that profit from our use of them. We can quit using them. Or, we can monkeywrench the norms of social media by sharing things that were never intended to be shared there, and see if it provokes more depth and thoughtfulness to permeate the platform.

Each approach has its benefits. I'm a fan of the former and have dramatically reduced my use of social media over the last three years. Instead of posting on Facebook or Instagram all the time, I like to text a picture to a friend who I think would like it. I save a lot of my big updates for phone calls or in-person get-togethers instead of throwing it onto the internet and seeking a few meager likes or comments in return.

Angelica in San Francisco is a fan of the latter approach. "I try to defy the social media [norms] by making my posts super intro-spective. I try to have deeper conversations online, even though it's not easy."[6] Julia Nguyen, a computer engineer and the founder of If-Me.org, an open source mental health app, takes the same approach. She does her part to upend the shallowness of social media by being open online about mental health, insecurities, and emotions like burnout, self-doubt, and frustration.[7] Her posts and articles are brave and raw and real.

Evaluate whether your use of social media is bringing you closer to the people in your world, or just giving you the illusion of closeness. When you look at the last five or ten people who liked, commented on, or reposted something that you shared, are they people you would feel comfortable calling on the phone right now to talk or asking them to come over for dinner tomorrow? What about the people whose posts you recently liked, commented on, or reposted? I'm not saying that we should all delete every social media app and never use them again (although I do think it might be healthy). However, I do encourage you to think about how and why you use social media the way you do. Don't just use it because it feels like you're supposed to. You have a choice. The hours you spend on social media can be used for anything you want. If you think your social media use is producing too many parasocial relationships in your life, work to change this. You deserve better. The next two Try Its will give you ideas that you can start using this week.

Go Behind the Scenes

When you find out a friend has recently returned from a trip (or got a new job, moved to a new city, etc.), ask your friend for the director's cut. Inquire about the details they haven't posted online. Ask questions about the things that don't make it into the photos: moments that were difficult or tinged by worry or moments that were just flat-out mundane. Ask about the conversations they've had recently. Ask what they've learned about themselves or about the world this year as a result of their experiences. Get curious. Go beyond the surface.

Do a Social Media Un-share

Version 1

The next time you want to share an update with all of your followers, pick one or two people that you think would be most interested in your news and tell them each directly instead.

Version 2

The next time a friend shares something on social media that you connect with or are curious about, instead of posting a comment, take the time to tell them directly, whether as a direct message, text message, voice memo, or IRL conversation. Want to hear more about their family visit, vacation, conference presentation, latest achievement, or recent struggle? Ask if they'll tell you about it over the phone or in person.

Version 3

For one month, instead of posting photos on Instagram, send each IG-worthy photo to only one person. Send it to them directly or show them the next time you see each other. If your photo isn't good enough to share with an audience of one, then why are you sharing it with all of your followers? See what happens if you go deep with one person instead of sharing photos indirectly with many people.

IMAGINARY FRIENDS

Over the last several years, I've become a podcast devotee. I listen to podcasts about five times a week, usually on my commute. I listen more often if I'm not also working my way through an audiobook. Podcasts fit flexibly around the other apparatus of daily life. I can listen while I ride the bus, while I exercise, while I'm cooking dinner or folding laundry. They're easy to access, fun, free, entertaining, informative, and they add value to my life. Just like good friends.

Half the US population above the age of twelve—about 167 million people—are podcast listeners.[1] It looks like some of us can't get enough. Our listening habits have made podcasts one of the fastest growing forms of media over the last several years. 32 percent of the US population listens to at least one podcast a month, and 22 percent listen to at least one podcast weekly. Younger demographics are especially avid listeners. In 2018, 30 percent of the twelve to twenty-four-year-old demographic had listened to a podcast in the last month. That number jumped to 40 percent in 2019.[2]

One day, while I was riding home from work listening to hosts Jen and Trin discuss a listener's question on the Friendshipping podcast, it occurred to me that what I was really listening to was a conversation between friends. I laughed at their jokes. I had follow-up questions and commentary of my own, albeit just in my head. I admired the way they bounced ideas and perspectives off each other. And I wondered if, in that moment,

I wasn't only listening because I was interested in the subject of the podcast, but because I wanted to "hang out" with some of my favorite podcasters. I haven't been able to shake the suspicion that there might be a connection between the meteoric rise in the popularity of podcasts and the simultaneous increase in rates of loneliness. Despite the fact that people have a harder time making conversation in their own lives, they're still hungry for it. Listening to other people have good conversation serves as a substitute for having our own.

It reminds me of the cuddle cafes and rent-a-family services I've heard about that you can hire in Japan when your real life is starved for touch and emotional support.[3] Only about half of Americans get to have meaningful in-person interactions, such as an extended conversation with a good friend, every day. Almost everyone else squeaks by, having on average one meaningful interaction per week, or per month. A small but meaningful 2 percent of people say they never get to engage with others.[4] I suspect that one reason for

the skyrocketing popularity of conversational podcasts is that they give us a chance to sit in on the kinds of conversations we wish we could have in real life with real friends. Podcasts are a no-risk way to siphon feelings of depth and connection to humans we wish were our actual friends—but without all the pesky performance anxiety. When you're just passively listening, you don't need to make any effort. But you also only get a fraction of the benefit of sharing a two-way connection.

Don't get me wrong. I'm not saying that listening to podcasts is a bad thing. I love podcasts. But there's no substitute for having a real conversation where you can share your thoughts, feelings, and experiences with someone who is listening to you, too. If you're into podcasts, let your listening be a catalyst for human connection instead of a replacement for it.

Friendcast

There's no need to stop listening to podcasts if they add value to your life. But see if you can find a way to balance your passive consumption by proactively pursuing conversation and connection, too.

For one month, use each podcast you listen to as a jumping off point for a conversation with one person in real life. Or ask a friend to listen to the same podcast episode before you talk. You could even ask people to come to a "Dinner Pod-dy" with a subject they want to talk about, such as the topic of a podcast they listened to, something they've read that had an impact on them, or something they wonder about. Subscribe to episodes of awesome real-life storytelling with the people you already know or want to know better.

ASK BETTER QUESTIONS

Getting together doesn't mean much if we waste the opportunity to make it matter. Alison Wood Brooks and Leslie K. John, professors at Harvard Business School, have explored how the power of asking the right questions can pull people closer together and increase depth and intimacy in relationships. A lot of people assume that small talk is necessary in relationships, that it absolutely must come first as a prerequisite warm-up to more personal topics. A limited amount of small talk can work well for building brand new relationships and is usually treated as the default first step for establishing connection, but it's not the only way. Depending on how open or closed off people are, small talk can actually inhibit closeness, especially if you get stuck there every time you have a conversation with someone. Small talk can become the destination instead of the on-ramp.

In their article "The Surprising Power of Questions," Brooks and John provide a guide for skillfully using inquiry to build rapport and relationships. They recommend using open-ended questions, paying careful attention to tone, and asking self-revelatory questions a bit earlier than you think is okay (because it's usually okay).[1]

Don't feel awkward doing this. Science is on your side. Their research confirms that asking lots of questions fosters learning and feelings of fondness between the asker and the askee. Of course, you need to be thoughtful, taking the type of question, sequencing, and framing into account. You don't want the other person to feel

like they're being drilled, so interject with your own thoughts too, especially when you frame questions.

And behold the beauty of the follow-up question. Like chaining yarn into the stitches of an intricately crocheted sweater, asking follow-up questions pulls you deeper and deeper into a beautifully-textured conversation. See how many follow-up questions you can ask before the other person changes the subject.

For example, my coworker Miles asked me one morning how my weekend was. I could have replied with a simple "it was pretty good." Instead, I told him that I worked on some projects at home. He followed up by asking if they were work projects or outside-of-work projects. I told him they were personal projects, such as setting up a special shelf with some sentimental objects and positive messages on it. He asked if I was a spiritual person. I said yes, kind of. He asked if I'd heard about a new shop that just opened in Oakland that had really nice candles, affirmation cards, and woowoo things like that. He pulled up their Instagram page to show me, and I loved it. Miles is generous with his curiosity and knows the power of the follow-up question. In that single five-minute conversation, we learned something meaningful and personal about each other—that we both have a slightly woowoo side—and in doing so, our friendship took on a new dimension.

Great follow-up questions will reference the details that the other person shared, but simple open-ended follow-up questions work well too. For example: "Can you say more about that?", "Can you give me an example?", or "How did that make you feel?" Even being purposefully silent—accompanied by a nod, eye contact, and a breath—can work as a follow-up, since it leaves a space that the other person will often fill with elaboration. Where can you try this in your own life? Do an experiment this week where you practice the art of asking follow-ups. Chain those questions. Knit a beautiful connection.

One reason people love the photo series Humans of New York and all of its copycat spinoffs is because it offers us the rare chance to experience a level of vulnerability and connection with people that we might otherwise not have access to in our daily lives, and certainly not with strangers. We can live vicariously through the portrait and its accompanying quote that immediately gives us a momentary feeling of kinship with another

HUMANS OF HERE AND NOW

THE THING I'D REALLY LIKE THE MOST WOULD BE IF THE PEOPLE THAT ARE ALREADY A PART OF MY LIFE ASKED ME THOUGHTFUL QUESTIONS AND TRIED TO GET TO KNOW ME BETTER LIKE YOU ARE, MR. RANDOM PHOTOGRAPHER GUY

human being. The thing that's missing in the photo though, is the question that was asked before the person in the portrait gave their candid and open answer.

These are questions that you're capable of asking too. You don't have to walk around the world talking to strangers to have moments like this. Imagine what would happen if you started asking new questions of the people right in front of you, who are already in your life. Imagine what would happen if you started inviting them to be your Humans of Here and Now.

Better Conversations Today

If you want to have better conversations but don't know where to begin, I have included several hundred conversation-starter questions at the back of this book that I wrote and compiled over the last few years. Begin by picking two or three that you really like and keep those in your back pocket so that you can pull them out at a time when you'd normally default to the usual small talk. Periodically, switch out those questions for new ones and see how your conversations get better in all parts of your life.

SO AWKWARD

For many people, the process of making friends can be summed up in one word: *awkward*. One woman in San Francisco told me, "I've lived on my street for over ten years but I didn't really talk to my neighbors until I got a dog. It's just too awkward and uncomfortable. But if you have a dog, you're suddenly allowed to talk to strangers and not seem creepy."[1]

This bums me out because life wasn't always this way. When I compare social interactions from my glory days in the '90s to now, it seems like everywhere I turn, people are less comfortable with spontaneous, uncurated interactions, conversations, and activities.

Over the last decade, Jack Shriner, a psychotherapist in Seattle specializing in cognitive-behavioral therapy, anxiety, depression, and mindfulness, has seen increasing numbers of adult clients dealing with the challenges of social anxiety. He spends a lot of time helping people deal with feeling restricted in life, cut off from other people, and fearful. A common treatment for fear-based problems is to encourage people to face their fear in gently scaffolded ways.

Having started his psychotherapy practice before smartphones were as ubiquitous as they are today, he subscribes to the notion that the Information Age has had a negative effect on people's ability to interact with each other in easy, relaxed ways. "Smartphones are making us more afraid to take chances socially,"[2] he told me. One cause he suspects is the overabundance of options

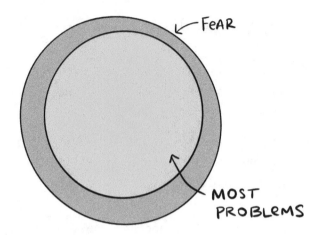

that the online world habituates us to expecting, and which can lead to procrastination or decision paralysis.

"People are in a compulsive act of seeing what their options are all day every day, but they never get themselves to go out and take the next step," he said. "For example, they might be texting someone for a month but never actually planning on meeting them in person." He doesn't see this as being a problem restricted to youth. He's seen the same behavior in a client who was in his seventies. "People are really compulsive with the constant checking of the phone, the constant scrolling, the constant what-if. And there's not a lot of taking action. There's fear there. Whether romantic or with friendship, it's a similar problem."

I told Shriner that in my interviews for this book, one word came up repeatedly when people described anything less than pleasant occurring in the realm of friendship. That word was: *awkward*. It surfaces when people describe their difficulty initiating

a friendship, navigating ambiguity, or handling conflict. "You nailed it," Shriner said. "Awkward is the word that people use the most. It's a catch-all for any form of discomfort or unease. Essentially, it all comes down to fear." The paradox, of course, is that to overcome it, you have to run towards it, not away from it. "If you're afraid of awkwardness, you have to seek out awkwardness. You have to show up for it with intention and say 'this is going to be awkward and I'm going to do it anyway.' Then you get used to it, and it's not so awkward any more." To help his clients get desensitized to awkwardness, he teaches them mindfulness techniques. He often leads clients through meditations and other exercises that can help them stay grounded when their anxiety bubbles up.

It also helps to replace the word "awkward" with a more discrete and specific emotion. "When people say, 'that would be awkward,' we explore which of the six basic emotions they're actually talking about feeling," Shriner says. "Is it happiness, sadness, fear, disgust, anger, or surprise? Awkward is vague. It doesn't mean that much. If you can replace it with a clearer emotion, then it's easier to suss out what your mind is really saying. If you're afraid, you can explore what you're afraid of. If you're sad, what are you sad about?" For decades, classic psychology has looked towards the six basic emotions that Shriner named; from there they fan out into many more nuanced feelings.[3] New research by Dacher Keltner, Professor of Psychology and Director of the Berkeley Social Interaction Lab at UC Berkeley, points to as many as 27 categories of emotion, all experienced on a spectrum of intensity.[4] Interestingly, Keltner's list includes Awkwardness as an emotion; due to his list's breadth, it also provides other distinct emotions that may actually be at play when we default to using 'awkward', such as Confusion, or Empathetic Pain. Learning to identify and express your emotions with greater specificity is key to navigating them successfully.

One person I met in my research who has wholeheartedly embraced the "feel the awkwardness and do it anyway" mantra that Shriner extols is Taylor, an artist in Sydney, Australia. Several years ago, she moved across the country with a romantic partner, leaving all of her friends and family behind in the process. Then they broke up and she realized she was all alone in Sydney since she hadn't done much to cultivate friendships there while she was coupled up.

Life in her new city felt like a blank slate, so she set out to meet people and make friends. Forging new friendships as an adult can sometimes feel hard because you start off not knowing anything about the other person's background or life. Taylor finds this mystery intriguing because as she says, "The other person is this magic ball of anything."[5] Unpeeling that mystery wasn't always easy for her. "People are often quite reserved as adults and their defense mechanisms can be quite strong."

Of course, there's still awkwardness, which she felt too. When it bubbled up, though, she was quick to notice that it was just her fear. "We fear running out of things to say. And the other person is also terrified of running out of things to say. But this isn't something to worry about. You're not really going to run out of things to say if you've made enough of an effort to get to know each other. You'll find things to talk about even if they're banal and strange. Just to be interested."

To get over her fear of social discomfort, she went all the way to ten on the awkwardness scale. Even though she had no prior experience, she started doing improvisational theatre. "Improv teaches you that you can fail miserably and fuck up and no one will do anything because they're also terrified about what they're doing," she told me over the phone. "I actually think that's really helped with vulnerability. It invites the other person to bring themselves totally: their weirdness, their off-the-wall-ness. For a year I was doing all of these improv courses and sticking with it and seeing the same twelve to twenty people. I became friendly with probably about six of them. And two of those are now people I would consider close friends."

Improv is inherently playful. Even when it's going badly, you're laughing about it. Taylor's choice to embrace playfulness in her attempts to overcome awkwardness and find friends proved to

"I've NeveR FeLT MoRe weiRD, oR moRe AccePTED."

be a winning strategy. So she sought it out in more places. "I also made some other friends through a board gaming night. I took myself there on my own, not knowing anyone. I knew it might be awkward, but I'd be around people and we'd have the excuse of *the thing we were doing*. Board games are really handy for that because there tends to be a lot of conversation around the table about the game. That makes it easier to see who people are and what they're like. At least you've got the game in common, and it's a sociable thing because you have to talk to each other."

After finding friends and connection via improv and board gaming, Taylor pushed herself again. "A step above board games is role-playing games—although it does take a certain kind of person, a level of confidence, and a willingness to make an ass of yourself," she laughed. "In role-playing games, you're not only talking socially, but you actually have to invent a world together.

I've made some of my strongest connections with people in that kind of interaction, even though they're people who I know very little about. We can create this entire imaginary world where it doesn't matter what we do for a living. I know who you are because I sat at the table with you and we've said, 'Okay, we might die. Got your bows and arrows? I've got my sword. Let's do this.' It's amazing what you'll find out about people, like their sense of humor or whether they're a team player. Role-playing games allow you to put on a mask and all you have to do is puppet this thing. The most fascinating part is that *most of the time people just play themselves*, but a slightly truer version of themselves. If you give people the opportunity to hide, they usually don't."

Taylor was successful in her search for friends as a result of dedicated action. First, she identified what her core hesitation was (fear). Then, she made an initial attempt to face her fear in a safe way (improv). When that was successful, she tried a new way (social board gaming), and when that went well, she took it a level further (role-playing games). Along the way, she saw how her feelings of awkwardness flew out the window when she wasn't focused on whether or not she felt awkward.

Taylor's a living, breathing example of what cognitive scientist and president of Barnard College, Sian Beilock, would love for us all keep in mind. In a February 2018 *New York Times* article called "Why Trying to Be Less Awkward Never Works," Beilock spoke about her book *Choke* and described how focusing on how you're performing in a social situation is exactly the thing that dooms you to performing worse.[6] Being focused on *trying to not be awkward* is basically guaranteed to make you feel, and seem, more awkward.

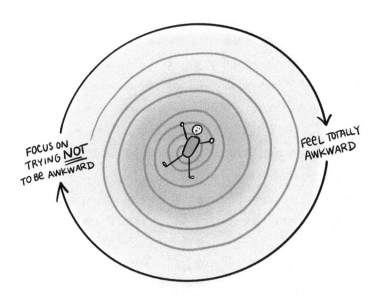

The way out of this conundrum, Beilock says, is to focus as much as you can on the other person. The more you focus on the other person or people that you're with, the more your brain has to give its attention to something other than you, and the more comfortable you're bound to feel. Our brains are not very adept at focusing on two things at once. By making it focus on the other person, we stop it from being overly focused on ourselves. Our reward for this shift in attention is feeling more at ease—oh and, bonus: having an easier time making friends.

Get Over Awkwardness

When it comes to trying new things or facing conversations that make us feel stressed out or uncomfortable, pithy inspirational missives like "Just Do It" can be too open-ended. Jack Shriner suggests breaking the task down into steps using a cognitive-behavioral treatment tool called the exposure hierarchy.[7]

How to do it:

- Write a list of all the things you could do to confront your fear or to address the situation that causes you to feel afraid.

- Rank the list from the scariest action to the easiest action, rating how much distress you predict this will cause you on a scale of one to ten (with ten being most distressing).

- In the following week, try the easiest one. Use mindfulness and breathing practices to help you stay grounded.

- Tackle every item on your list one by one until you get to the action that's hardest. You don't have to go in order— experiment with jumping around on the list.

You can try this technique for anything you're afraid of, whether that be signing up for a new class, asking a new friend to coffee, or having an uncomfortable conversation with a friend about something that's gone wrong in your friendship. In time, you'll learn that you can tolerate the situation you found stressful, and then apply that learning to your future actions.

Get to Know Your Feelings and Needs

Being able to accurately identify and then communicate our true feelings is key to handling them in a healthy way. We are also better friends to others when we can be specific about how we feel, and why.

The Center for Non-Violent Communication provides an exhaustive list of feelings and needs, with over 200 specific feelings to pick from. Their list also categories feelings into two groups: when our needs are being met, and when our needs are not being met. The feelings list is meant to be used on conjunction with their list of needs, to help people have clearer and more compassionate communication about how they feel and what they would like to request from others.

Find each list at:

www.cnvc.org/training/resource/feelings-inventory

www.cnvc.org/training/resource/needs-inventory

For more resources, check out *Nonviolent Communication: A Language of Life* by Marshall B. Rosenberg for skill-building tips on identifying emotions and responding compassionately in any situation.

I've also included a handy chart of feelings in the appendix on page 262 that you can use to practice identifying and communicating your feelings to others.

Magic Ball of Anything

Curiosity is a skill and it needs to be practiced. Exercise your curiosity by looking up a list of events, classes, and happenings in your town. Sites like Eventbrite, CourseHorse, and Dabble are a good place to start. If your city isn't listed on those sites, then turn to your local alternative newsweekly. Pick out seven events or classes that appeal to you. The first few can be things that you're already familiar or comfortable with. I love art so I'd probably pick things in this category like checking out an art exhibit or attending an art class. The last few things you pick should be a stretch for you—things that you're not familiar with or not already super comfortable doing. For me, this might involve going to a board gaming cafe or any kind of fitness class involving the word "bootcamp." Remember, the goal is to practice nonjudgmental curiosity in each of these events you go to.

Each experience, and the people you meet there, will be your magic ball of anything. If someone interests or intrigues you, strike up a conversation. You already have one thing in common: you both came to this class or event. Ask about them, tell them about you. The purpose isn't necessarily to leave with a new bestie. It's to let yourself be curious about the world and other people in it. What you learn in the process is your reward.

5-4-3-2-1

Another way to move past feelings of awkwardness in a social situation is to shift your focus from yourself to your surroundings. It doesn't even require talking to anyone else; it's all done silently in your own head. Here's how to do it.

First, take a deep breath and turn your attention outward. Using your powers of observation, notice:

- Five things you can see
- Four things you can hear
- Three things you can feel
- Two things you can smell (or could smell if you got closer)
- One thing you can (or would like to) taste

Simply focusing on your senses and the environment you're in can help you feel more balance and peace. As you begin to feel more at ease, think about who you'd like to speak to or approach. Then give more of your relaxed attention to the person or people that you're with.[8]

FACE THE MUSIC

Even in wonderful friendships, it's not always butterflies and sunny days. Disagreements, misunderstandings, arguments, hurt feelings, and disappointments can all still happen. It's how we deal with these situations that matters.

Good friends don't ghost when something goes wrong in a friendship. But sadly, disappearing after a conflict is becoming a norm for many people because fixing it is too painful to bear, they lack the skills to fix it, or they just don't care. After a screw up, it's often too hard for many people to reach out and say, "I want to apologize. Can we talk about what happened?" Instead, a lot of people walk away from a friendship entirely rather than deal with the awkwardness (a.k.a. difficult emotions like anger, sadness, and fear) or the discomfort of conflict resolution.

Conflict resolution can be especially uncomfortable for anyone who is scared to share unrehearsed thoughts in real time, and our devices make it so that we don't have to. Jack Shriner, the psychotherapist we met a few pages ago, described one common way that device dependency becomes especially pernicious when conflicts arise. "When facing potential conflicts, people feel safer typing out a five-page thesis about what their disagreement is, preemptively touching on every possible response that the other person could have,"[1] he told me. "The technology makes it easy to hide. You can type it out so you don't have to experience the uncertainty of an actual conversation," he said, noting that this is not a healthy coping strategy, nor one that fosters the trust, vulnerability, and honesty that are necessary to maintain a healthy friendship.

Ella, a teacher in Denver, described how two of her friendships went up in smoke due to this kind of conflict-avoidant behavior.[2] In the first situation, a long-term friend we'll call Debbie begged for an invitation to Ella's brother's ornate Indian wedding. Ella had to plead with her family to include her friend. Multiple family members made concessions to allow for Debbie's inclusion and comfort, including giving up their preferred overnight housing so Debbie could stay the weekend. Her name was even being carved into an elaborate wooden seating chart along with everyone else's. Then, at 11 p.m. the night before the wedding, Debbie sent Ella a text and bailed. Instead of driving a few hours to come to the wedding the next day, she had decided to stay home with her housemates and interview potential roommates from Craigslist. She had alluded the day prior that she might do this, and Ella had begged her to please show up, even offering to give Debbie money to cover rent if a suitable roommate couldn't be secured.

Debbie's text was apologetic and acknowledged that Ella would be upset. But it wasn't enough. "She didn't send a card, a gift, an apology to my parents, a phone call, nothing. She didn't even send a 'How was the wedding?' text afterwards," Ella told me. "There was no empathy, no 'How can I make this right?' She just texted and ghosted. She was probably the only friend I've made after high school who I would have called a best friend. That was in 2015. We haven't spoken since."

In the second situation, Ella's neighbor, who we'll call Janey, pressured her into having a bachelorette party weekend even though that wasn't a priority for Ella in advance of her own wedding. Offering to plan and lead everything, it was also Janey's idea for a few of Ella's friends to fly in from out of state. She thought it would be fun for them to join the festivities with Ella, Janey, and a few other neighborhood friends. Refusing to accept assistance with planning over the next five weeks, Janey said she'd do it all on her own.

During that time, she hemmed and hawed and promised to send updates that never materialized. The morning after Ella's friends flew into town, Janey sent them all an email saying, "I hope you have a great weekend. I made you guys a reservation for brunch. Sorry but I'm not going to be able to make it." A couple of Ella's neighbors also sent flaky texts saying they weren't coming. Janey's absence was the most egregious since she had taken responsibility for planning the entire event. Ella texted back saying how disappointed she was, how much she wished that Janey would have called her instead of bailing over email. She expressed that she was too upset to see Janey at this moment so it was fine that she wasn't coming, but Ella emphasized that she didn't want this to be the end of their friendship.

Janey's response was a four-paragraph text full of excuses about how she's not as organized as Ella, and which culminated in this friendship-severing comment: "Your feelings about this are your problem, not mine. My friendship and integrity have been questioned. There's nothing more to be said." Ella replied, saying that she wanted to patch things up and hoped to spend time with Janey over the holidays. Janey didn't respond. Despite the fact that they live three doors down from each other, Ella and Janey

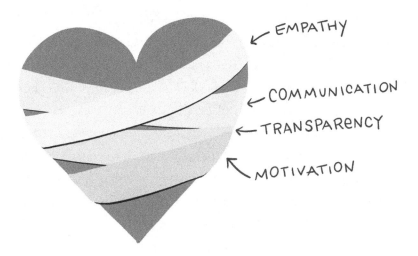

never spoke again. It's true that Ella could have tried harder to seek repair by calling Debbie or Janey when they hadn't called her, or by going in person to Janey's house, but her friends weren't meeting her halfway. The other person has to want to make it right, too.

Being let down by her friends in these situations clarified Ella's definition of friendship, which is similar to the view held by the Marvel and DC Comics writer Len Wein. He spent most of his life writing stories about the alliances, trials, and tribulations of dozens of superheroes and villains, most famously the X Men. Wein once said, "A true friend is someone who is there for you when he'd rather be anywhere else." His superheroes' allegiance to each other is the same kind of dedication that Ella hopes to share in her friendships, and that she realized she'd never get from Debbie and Janey. Ella said through tears that these friendship flame-outs showed her the four things that need to be in place for a friendship rift to heal: communication, transparency, empathy, and mutual motivation to repair the friendship. I agree with her.

With those qualities in place, it's possible to heal even deep disappointments. Empathy—compassionately putting yourself in the other person's shoes—is fundamental. Also, conflict resolution requires a suitable method of communication. Text messages and emails are not a replacement for phone calls or face-to-face conversations. One of the best ways to make sure that our friendships survive injury is to practice being more self-aware, skillful, and considerate friends ourselves. The tips on the next two pages will help you do just that.

Be a Better Listener

If something has gone sideways in your friendship, ask your friend to tell you what they're feeling and thinking. Then be quiet and listen. Resist the urge to interrupt, defend, or answer back. Let them get out everything they need to say. After you clarify that you've understood them correctly by repeating back what you heard, ask, "Is it okay if I respond?" Start by sharing your feelings, then your reflections. You can both use the feelings chart on page 262 to help you identify your feelings and express them compassionately.

Give Better Apologies

Jamie Utt, an author and diversity and inclusion consultant, writes on *Everyday Feminism* that the best apologies are ones in which the apologizer focuses on the impact on their actions and resists the urge to frame their message around their intentions, regardless of how harmless they were. Remember that an apology should be focused on the person who has been hurt, not the one who did the hurting. If you hurt your friend, what actually matters is their pain, not the preservation of your reputation as a good person.[4]

Apologize, reflect, ensure that you understand the other person fully, and empathize to the best of your ability. When you make an apology, don't say "I'm sorry *if* you felt ____" or even "I'm sorry you feel that way." These are not apologies, they're deflections of responsibility. Start with the truth, and end on your intention to do better. "I'm sorry that I ____ and that it led to ____. In the future, I'll ____ so this doesn't happen again."

If you want to practice this skill in a lower-stakes way, talk to a friend about something that happened in the past that you could have done a better job apologizing for. Try giving them a better apology using your new skills now. Building up your muscle memory for giving better apologies will help you the next time you need to apologize for real.

ASK FOR HELP

Olivia is a fifty-something therapist who got divorced ten years ago, which set off a chain of events that turned her life upside down for a while. On the coattails of her divorce, she decided to end her career as a nurse and go to graduate school. At work she'd been lucky to have a fair number of friends who she could see and check in with on a daily basis, but they largely went away when the job did. The social circle she'd been a part of when she was married was primarily made up of people who were her ex's friends. So when they split up, she also lost her friend community. "I lost a lot of social groups that I had been a part of. Those changes set me up for a difficult five years where I was struggling with who I was and who my friends were,"[1] she explained to me.

During that five years, Olivia moved three times. Even though all her moves were within the same region, they were still very disruptive. In the midst of all this, she also decided to change her religion and spirituality practice. She left the Quaker community she'd been a part of and joined a meditation community instead. There, she found a women's group and hit the friendship jackpot. She keeps in touch with this group of women over group text and sees them in person at least a few times a month. "I make friends where my biggest orientation is in life, and for me, that's often been spiritual organizations," she told me.

Many of the women in the group have proven to be lifelines for her. Several months before Olivia and I spoke, her mother died.

The women in her meditation circle were the support system she called on. "I remember walking up and down the airport sobbing, and I called my friend Celeste without hesitation. I could speed-dial probably five to ten different women and say 'my mom died' and they would be there to take my call."

While Olivia was away tending to family business and having a hard time with some of the decisions that family members were making, she reached out to one of the women from her meditation circle. On one particularly hard day, she asked that friend to meditate with her over the phone. It was so helpful they ended up doing it again for the next four days. When she got back in town and was still grieving, one friend came over, sat with her, and listened for hours. Another friend offered her an open door to come over any time.

"She's a mom with two kids under twelve, and she still said I could show up at her house any time. One day around Christmas when I was really sad I just knocked on her door and said 'I'm feeling sad, I'm thinking about my mom, my birthday is tomorrow, and I need a hug.' Immediately, she and her two kids just embraced me as I was crying. Afterwards I sat on the couch and her little dog jumped on my lap and I sat there and watched the kids play for an hour while we drank tea." Olivia's friend provided so much, so simply. All it took was an open door, open arms, and a spirit of loving openness.

On another hard occasion, a different friend showed up for her in a major way. Olivia's menopause transition was so intense that she started having panic attacks. One night a panic attack came on as she was driving home. Sobbing in her car, unable to drive,

IN CASE OF EMERGENCY

BREAK DOWN YOUR
EMOTIONAL WALLS
AND CALL A FRIEND

she pulled over and called Grace, one of the friends from her circle. Even though Grace had been relaxing at home with her husband and kids, she drove to the gas station where Olivia was parked to be with her.

"It was 9 o'clock at night and she was there for me. She got in my car at the gas station and she sat with me. She let me sob and talk and sob and talk, and then about an hour later, we were laughing. She encouraged me to take sick time, which I never feel like I can do." Grace helped Olivia see that she needed and deserved the sick time and that it was possible to take a week off to care for herself.

Olivia's connection with her friends is marked by a remarkable amount of vulnerability, reciprocity, acceptance, and adaptability. This became evident on some of her darkest days and also shows up in smaller ways. "Even though I'm not a runner, when a few of the women started training for a half marathon, I wanted to support them. So I started going along with them to warm up and train even though I had no intention of running a half marathon. We would do push ups, squats, and go for short runs. I went every Saturday with them. Afterwards we'd have lunch and spend time with their kids. I made a few deep heart friends—like two or three best friends—out of that."

With deep dedication, Olivia showed up, often driving for over an hour each way to be in the presence of the friends she loved. She tagged along on their marathon training because that's what it took to support the friends who had been so supportive to her.

The cycle of generous asking and generous receiving are a huge part of her life. Once, when Olivia was in the airport flying home to deal with family affairs after her mother's death, she found a young woman crying in the bathroom. It was the young woman's first time traveling alone; she'd lost her credit card and her flight was cancelled. Although Olivia herself was in a time of need, she listened to that young stranger talk through her problems and then they figured out a solution together. Just because you need help doesn't mean that you can't also give it. As she sees it, "There's just something special about people helping each other."

Olivia and her friends are making their ancestors proud. Throughout human history, people have had to be constantly and cooperatively involved with each other—to hunt and prepare food, to build shelter, to raise children, to care for the elderly, to learn and be entertained, to overcome adversity, and to celebrate triumph. Staying alive through the ages has been a constantly humbling practice of enlisting other people's help, and getting involved in whatever they're trying to accomplish too.

Today, millions of people feel like they don't have anyone to lean on—not for the big life stuff that Olivia was dealing with, nor for the small things like navigating the world and making day-to-day decisions. I mean, think about it: if you live in a modern city and you have a credit card and an internet connection, you don't really need to ask anyone for help. Google Maps gives you directions. Yelp offers recommendations. Google can serve up advice and answers for nearly everything. You can make your own professional connections on LinkedIn. Public and private transportation gets you where you need to go. You hardly ever need to ask another person directly for help with anything. This is amazing and terrible. It's like we're in a race to prove that we can make other humans unnecessary.

If you're not in the habit of developing relationships that foster intimacy and reciprocal care, who will you turn to on a hard day when you just want a hug and to be listened to while you cry it out? There's no app for that. I've sometimes thought that being self-sufficient and not asking people for help makes me a better friend. A participant in a workshop I held described feeling the same way. "I hate to feel like I'm inconveniencing people,"[2] she said. In my twenties, I used to ask friends for help with all kinds of things: moving, rides, ideas, recipes, building stuff, you name it. Nowadays, not so much. I question that change and wonder if it makes my life and my friendships better or worse.

No one wants to be thought of as overly needy. But the downside of being too self-sufficient is that it can impede connection. If we don't ask for help, we don't give other people a chance to share their gifts with us, and vice versa. We don't show them our weaknesses, or our imperfect humanness. We miss out on the chance to deepen our connection by showing our friends that we're there for them, too.

Julia, the engineer and founder that we met earlier, described how much she values reciprocity with the friends she feels comfortable confiding in. "Being someone with mental illness, I really appreciate being checked on. I also appreciate if [my friends] share things about themselves. When you have mental illness, oftentimes you worry that you're treating your friend like a therapist if you're just dumping information about all the things you're dealing with. It can feel like you're being a burden on your friends. In the friendships where I share things about my mental illness, I also tell that friend that they can open up to me and share however much they want to as well. It would be cool if more of my friends knew that they could share their troubles with me, and I would try my best to listen and be supportive too."[3]

Beth Barany, a novelist and writing coach, is unabashed about asking for professional help from one of her closest friends. "We're fans of each other and we're also professionals who are really honestly helping each other—whether it's giving each other feedback on our writing, or strategic feedback like 'let me be honest with you about your strengths and weaknesses.'"[4] Beth fully embraces the fact that asking for help means admitting that we don't know something, or that we can't do something by ourselves. "I'm excited about having more conversations with people where I don't know something that they know, because that's the edge of my knowledge and understanding."

Asking for help didn't always come easy for Beth. "Years ago I had a repetitive stress injury in my forearms, and I couldn't lift anything, not even a piece of paper. I had to get over my pride and ask for help. That was a huge lesson for me. I got used to being more soft and more vulnerable. My injury taught me the value of asking for help."

You don't have to wait to ask for help until you're facing the biggest challenges of your life, like divorce, death, mental illness, or injury. Even small moments of vulnerability can build intimacy and closeness. My friend Linda recalled having a pretty intense allergy attack at home last Independence Day. It wasn't serious enough to go to the hospital, but her eyes had puffed shut and she was sneezing uncontrollably. She was miserable. She didn't have any allergy medicine, and all the stores near her were closed for the holiday.

Thinking about who she could ask for help, she remembered that a woman she had taken a yoga teacher training with lived in her neighborhood. So Linda called her acquaintance, who did have some Benadryl on hand and was happy to swing by with it. The encounter reignited their connection and inspired them to stay in touch more frequently. If Linda hadn't had the gumption to reach out and ask for help, she would have suffered alone. Reaching out brought physical relief and it connected her to a new friend in her neighborhood.[5]

Vulnerability can also be expressed in the form of radical generosity, as I learned from a retiree named Marian. Her own children and grandchildren are grown up and off living their lives. They don't call or visit very often, so Marian found a gap in her life that her grandmotherly duties used to fill. She still felt the desire to offer the kind of caring, supportive listening, and life advice that good grandmas are known for giving. So she created an account on the app NextDoor, a social network for neighborhoods. Marian offered her volunteer services as a surrogate grandma. She welcomed anyone who felt they didn't get enough grandmotherly support from their own biological grandmothers, those whose grandmas had passed away, and moms and kids who didn't have access to grandmothers in their local area. As a result, she met a couple other women who became friends and surrogate granddaughters. With a mix of creativity, courage, and kindness, Marian added more companionate support to her own life while also enriching the lives of others.[6]

Functional social support usually comes in one of four ways: Emotional, tangible, informational, and companionate.[7] Emotional support (a.k.a. esteem support or appraisal support) looks like giving someone love, affection, acceptance, caring, empathy, and other behaviors that foster mutually positive feelings. Tangible support is concrete and direct, like helping someone move from one apartment to another, giving them money, or making them meals. Informational support includes giving advice, recommendations, introductions, and practical solutions. Companionate support is given and received when we are present with each other in ways that contribute to feelings of belonging, like showing up to celebrate someone's birthday, visiting them when they're in the hospital, or sitting together when you know they're having a hard day. Receiving support when we need it matters, and what's interesting is that

I'M HERE FOR YOU, FRIEND.

some researchers have found that it matters even more to simply know that support would be there for you, even if you rarely ever call upon it.

When you feel like you need to ask a friend for support, look inside to identify what type of support you need. When you ask for help, try to be specific about what kind of help you want. It can be frustrating to speak to a friend about a problem when we want emotional support (listening, nurturance, empathy) yet the other person starts offering informational support (advice, suggestions, solutions). Similarly, offer your friends the range of support, and ask them what they need, too.

Giving and receiving help in your friendships benefits your mental health and physical health in just about every way you can imagine.[8] It all begins with having the courage to make a humble request. Embrace radical vulnerability in your asking and practice effusive generosity in your giving. It will help you develop trust and mutuality in your friendships and in all areas of your life.

Check Your Safety Nets

The US Fire Administration recommends checking your home's smoke detectors once a month and replacing the batteries twice a year when you change your clocks.[9] That's because vital safety equipment needs to be checked regularly when things are going fine to ensure that it will work in a crisis. Friends are also vital to our safety and wellbeing. Have you checked the batteries on your friendships? Do you know who you can count on in a time of need? Who would pick up the phone and be there for you when you need them most? Now's a great time to have those conversations. Start by asking a friend or two who they would call in a time of need. Let them know that you'd be there for them, and ask if it's okay for you to reach out to them too. A great lead-in to the conversation is to share stories about a time when you each received or gave help to other people.

Go Old School

Have you noticed the way that internet culture has made it seem like it's rude to ask another person a question that is google-able? Computers full of answers are training us to rely on each other less and less. Do an experiment where you turn that norm on its head. For one week, every time you think about looking something up online, ask someone instead. You can tell them about your experiment so they don't think you're a total weirdo. Ask them if they know the answer—and they're not allowed to look on the internet either. Have a conversation about it. Share your best guesses. Have the conversations you would have if the internet was down. See if life feels any different when you try connecting to people more and relying on your phone less.

Extra Credit

• *See your world:* Try to navigate through the world using your memory or intuition. Don't look at Google Maps. If you get lost, figure it out, or pretend that you're a tourist whose phone has a dead battery and ask a human to help you find your way.

• *Be adventurous:* For three months, don't read any reviews of restaurants, bars, or stores before you go to them. This sounds like a long time, but the point is to break the habit of relying on the internet to guide your every step. If you want a suggestion, ask a person.

• *Untether yourself:* Ask someone what time it is or use an old-school watch instead of checking the time on your phone.

FROM FRIENDSHIP to COMMUNITY

It's a foggy Saturday in December with mist hanging softly in the mid-morning air. I'm walking up to a cheerful shingle-sided house flaunting huge sprays of rosemary and bright orange torch lilies in front. Colorful mosaics patched together from painted tiles and chipped pottery line the walkway, and a bright green wisteria arbor welcomes me. In a corner of the yard, there's a wrought iron cafe table with five empty chairs circling it. On the table, a small pile of well-worn gardening gloves wait patiently for their next adventure in the soil. I hear the sound of water softly trickling from a combination fountain-irrigation system that runs at the edge of an abundant garden. I'm here to have tea with Jeannie.

Jeannie and I met recently at a women's meetup in Berkeley. After I mentioned that I was working on a book about adult friendship and community, she approached me and said she'd love to share her experiences. There was a sparkle in her eye and she was clearly excited to talk. I was intrigued because, unlike a lot of people I mention this project to, Jeannie didn't immediately launch into lamentations about what a challenge it is to find friends and community as an adult. Quite the contrary. Jeannie said her life is absolutely full of friendship and community and she wanted to share her story about how it came to be that way.

Jeannie has had an amazing life marked by a high degree of autonomy and independence. Her last job working for someone else was in food service at age nineteen. She's worked for herself ever since and is in her late fifties now. Never one to shy away from risk or adventure, as a young adult she hitchhiked alone across the country—twice. With rare exception, she's been living communally for more than thirty years. She's the founder and central member of a six-person communal household.

She welcomed me to her home with a warm hug. As we were getting situated for our chat, we crossed paths with a few other women: one was a housemate who enthusiastically invited me to learn more about her project focused on local textiles and fabric-making; another was a friend who had swung by to help clean up the garden; then we chatted with two other friends who were picking up a recording of a guided meditation from Jeannie. In my first fifteen minutes there, I observed a flow of people in her home that seemed relaxed, happy, and effortless; some of them lived there and some didn't, but they all moved with such ease through the house, that the difference was undecipherable. At her large dining table, Jeannie and I settled down with mugs of tea and dove into conversation about how her existing community came to be and her views on how to cultivate strong friendships and community.

"This house has been an evolution. I've lived in communal households since my daughter was five years old, and now she's thirty-six—so thirty-one years. I've always had at least one other person I was living with. Her father and I broke up after she was conceived but we stayed housemates until she was five. That was our deal so she'd have a solid place and not have to go back and forth. It was *her* house and we went back and forth. When she was a little older, I moved into a communal household."[1] In the process, she made many short term and long term friends.

Jeannie emphasized that community doesn't just happen spontaneously. To succeed, a community usually needs a structure of some kind. For example, her current group house has a three-month trial period for anyone who moves in. For those who stay, there are shared agreements for future engagement. "In all the houses I've lived in, we had meetings or shared food. Here we have a house meeting once a month and we share food, conversation, kitchen time, and projects. We instigate each other's creativity. Food is a really great way to bring cohesion. And we bring structure to our house meetings too; everybody has time to check in, we make a meal together, and we have an agenda of things we want to talk about. There's a lot of openness and joy in our conversations and gatherings together. We all have a pretty strong lack of attachment to personal position—everyone has a lot of flexibility regardless of seniority. And as the holder of the house, it's my job to have that flexibility more than anybody. I want it to be a place where everyone feels like they get to have their creativity and self-expression, even if it's not always easy for me. It's important that there be good facilitation, either a person who holds that role or an agreed-upon process.

"I also believe in raising kids with a lot of adults around, especially for teenagers—they need guidance but they don't want it from their parents. When my daughter was born, I would bring her to collective meetings and she would get passed around. I think about how many babies don't have that. It's so hard for the parents. And for the child who grows up like that, how can they trust the world? So as a parent, I felt like my job was to facilitate who the adults were around her." As a result of Jeannie's open

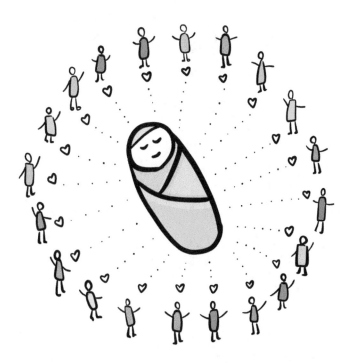

parenting style, her daughter has loving kin-like relationships with multiple adults who are a part of both their lives.

Jeannie's home bubbles over with cozy friendliness and tenderness permeates her interactions with the people passing through. This is the exception rather than the norm for most people. In the United States, there are more people living alone now than ever before.[2] Jeannie doesn't think it's necessary to live communally in order to experience strong community. She does think it's easier if you live with others, but cultivating meaningful friendship and community has less to do with the format of your home and more to do with how you show up in the world.

"You have to ask yourself, 'What is my life *for*? Is my life about consuming resources and having whatever I want, or is my life a

gift to the world?'" She encourages people to say to themselves: "I was born as a gift to the planet. How am I sharing that gift?"

To those who don't know what their gifts are or how to share them, she quotes Howard Thurman: "Don't ask what the world needs. Ask what makes you come alive, and go do it. Because what the world needs is people who have come alive."

"What brings you life? What brings you joy? Go connect with people from that place, and there's your community. Is it food? Music? That place of love is your higher place. It doesn't matter if you're an introvert or an extrovert. Ask what brings you into your creative place. And get comfortable with yourself. It's taken me a long time and I'm in a pretty good place 95 percent of the time. You weave together a basket of community. It takes time to find your people, to experiment, and to get to know yourself. All these different people are opportunities—it gives you a sounding board for discovering your truth. A lot of times you find your truth by finding what's your not-truth. If you look at life as *school*, it's a lot easier. Every relationship and every community is that—all these possibilities for learning."

Because Jeannie is so immersed in the positivity of a life overflowing with friendship and community, it can be easy to assume that it was always this way for her. But it wasn't. Her life didn't follow any traditional paths, and her lessons were hard-won.

"I was always rebellious and I've always been a seeker. I was always on the outside of the in crowd. I didn't have community when I was a kid. I was weird, I didn't have very many friends. High school was depressing and I was suicidal when I got to college. I was bulimic and it was really intense, I was not valuing myself. I dropped out of college when I was seventeen, and I didn't end up graduating until I was forty. I was like, 'I'm doing life.' I taught violin lessons. I took a job at a cross-country ski lodge even though I'd never been on skis. I hitchhiked across the country, then I hitchhiked back."

Her adventures usually worked out fine, though she was once assaulted. Looking back on it now, she's even able to have compassion for the person who hurt her. In her perspective, it wouldn't have happened if he knew how to seek intimacy in a healthy way. She wistfully adds, "I had a lot of trust." Wanting to stay safe doesn't mean we shouldn't trust others. We just need to remember that the world we encounter will not always be the one that we want or deserve. But that's no reason to close ourselves off from others.

Half the population of our country now says they feel alone or left out most of the time. Loneliness is an uncomfortable place.

But even in this, there are valuable lessons to learn, she says. "Being alone, you learn how to love yourself. How to hold yourself. How to be compassionate with yourself. How to be in this container that you're in. When we feel isolated, it's because we don't understand that we're all connected. That isolation takes us into the depth of our own darkness. But it's a test when we look into that place of our darkness. There's a depth of creativity in that place. That's what brings movement. It can be inspiring." If we allow it to be.

Don't sit in that darkness forever, though. A single friend is the first place to start. From there, you build. "[Community is] connections between connections. If we're in community, then I'm sharing my people with you and you're sharing your people with me. There's more support in that. It's not as brittle [as a one-to-one connection]. Ask a friend to introduce you to someone else they love. Having community takes care of isolation, loneliness, jealousy, a lot of things—there's more fluidity and there's safety in it."

And no, you don't have to move into a big communal house to find it. "This isn't for everybody. There's different styles and everyone needs to find what their style is. There's the one-on-one style. But me, I like the big conversation. I open myself to so much. I'm greedy, I want to do all of life! I thrive on that."

Towards the end of our interview, we were interrupted by two travelers who had been staying at Jeannie's house and were departing for the next leg of their journey. Their goodbye was a spontaneous eruption of gratitude and joy with six arms wreathed in a long and loving group hug. You never would have guessed

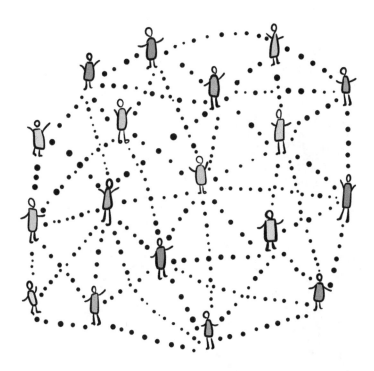

that they only met a week and a half before. It looked like the kind of heartfelt connection that exists between close friends or family members.

"That's one thing I love about this house. People come and go. For a while we had roommates that didn't want any subletters or short-term people staying here. It was lovely, like a little coven. But then different people moved in, and now there's much more openness. We can have quiet and solitude in our rooms, but then we can come out and instantly have community and warmth."

We should all be so lucky.

Next Level:
HOW TO ACCELERATE
ANY FRIENDSHIP

ZeRO TO SIXTY
IN TWO WeeKS

A few years ago I came up with a strategy that I call The QQ10 Method. The two Q's stand for Quality+Quantity, and the 10 stands for ten days. My hypothesis was that if two people who have decent chemistry commit to ten consecutive days of quality time, then they'll be able to form the kind of closeness that typically takes months to build. When I was using dating apps, I even posed this challenge in my profile and had a couple takers. Each time, it worked wonderfully. In two week's time, we could log enough hours of shared togetherness to make us feel like we'd known each other for way longer. The same thing can happen for platonic friendships that we want to supercharge from the get-go.

How it works

For ten days straight, you and the other person see each other and communicate daily, as much as comfortably possible. It can be face to face or by phone or video call. The goal is sustained immersion. You can do big things like seeing a show or taking a class together, or you can do tiny things like grocery shopping, cooking, sharing a meal, or sitting in a park to people-watch and talk about life. You'll be using all four Seeds of Connection by sharing proximity, immersing yourself in frequency, developing and exploring your compatibility, and demonstrating your commitment. This provides you with:

Momentum

Just like the formation of any other habit, you don't have to try as hard to do something once you perceive it as a regular part of your life.

Continuity

There's no big start or stop to the conversation. You just keep going. You don't have to spend a ton of time reorienting to each other every time you reconnect. You establish a flow where you can pick up where you left off—a key characteristic of true friends.

Authenticity

Anyone can perform well on a date—romantic or platonic—especially when you have days, weeks, or months in between hangouts and you're only seeing each other for a couple hours each time. But when you connect daily and in a wide variety of activities, the real you is bound to come through. So you get to know each other for who you really are, not the shiny Instagram-worthy version of you that cleans up for selfies and friend-dates.

Familiarity

Even if the experiment is a wash and you decide you're not going to be BFFs, I bet that whenever you see each other again, there's going to be an easy air of casual familiar energy in your interactions from that moment forward. Not bad for less than two weeks of effort, right?

THE FRIENDSHIP INCUBATOR

Do you have a Friend Lite that you want to level up? Have you checked to make sure you both want to create a closer friendship with each other? Are you each willing to give this the kind of committed attention that you'd give to finishing several seasons of *Grey's Anatomy* or *Game of Thrones*?

If the answer to all three of the above questions is yes, and you're looking for something more intensive, I suggest trying The Friendship Incubator. First, pinkie-swear that you're each going to give it your best shot, then dive in. Here's what it looks like:

90 days

Pick a start date and an end date three months later. Put it in both your calendars. You'll also be putting some other stuff in your calendar (see below), but clearly mark the beginning and the end of your incubator window. You don't need to wait for the first day of a month. You can start whenever you both agree is good.

12 hangout minimum

Aim to get together *at least* twelve times during your three-month window. If you can't do twelve, don't give up—aim for eleven or ten. More is ok but absolutely no less than twelve. Yes, be nerdy and put it in both of your calendars, whether your preference is to schedule loosely or strictly (I recommend both). NO cancelling plans unless you're in bed with the flu. Actually, you can still hang out if you get sick. The other person brings soup, tea, and funny movies. Dedication is the name of the game.

Switch it up

Vary your activities. Do at least three different kinds of things together. For example, don't always go to the movies, don't always go to dinner, don't always go to happy hour, etc. Of course you can repeat things that are convenient and fun, but aim for variety. Make sure you choose activities that at least one of you is pumped for (though obviously it's better if you're both excited about it).

Get out

Do at least two exciting things together like attending an unusual workshop that neither one of you has done before, going to a concert by a band you both love, or taking a day trip to someplace neither one of you has been before.

Stay in

Spend time in each other's homes at least twice each. Don't worry about making your home into some kind of picture-perfect palace. You're not "entertaining" or "hosting"—you're hanging out. Relax. Do "boring" things together like laundry, cooking, pulling weeds, sitting on the couch eating chocolate, or talking while one of you organizes your closet. You don't need to have a plan in advance for your stay-home hangouts. They can even happen spontaneously. If you want, one of your at-home visits can also be your scheduled heart-to-heart.

Have a Heart Time

This is a heart-to-heart conversation with some guide rails on it for people who otherwise find it hard to be vulnerable or open up emotionally. If neither of you are prone to spontaneously sharing about personal or emotional topics, scheduling a Heart Time gives you a special setting to do it intentionally. It's time-boxed so if this is super uncomfortable for you, you know it won't last all night. If you and your friend are already super comfortable having heart to heart talks, feel free to skip to the next page. How it works:

• Get a timer and go to a place where you both feel comfortable and won't be interrupted. Decide who's going to speak first.

• The first person gets ten minutes to share something that they're struggling with, having a hard time with, frustrated by, embarrassed to talk about, secretly excited about, or otherwise keeping inside. The entire ten minutes are theirs; if they say they're done talking after five minutes, then sit in silence for the remaining five minutes, or they can take a break then speak some more until their time is up. The listener's job is to listen deeply for that first ten minutes—minimize questions and interruptions, and don't butt in with anecdotes about yourself. Listen as patiently and empathetically as you can.

• After the first person has talked for ten minutes, they should say what kind of feedback they want: advice, suggestions, silence, thoughtful questions, back and forth conversation, etc. Set the timer for ten minutes and share feedback. Then reset the timer and switch roles.

• After both of you have spoken, and given feedback, debrief by talking about how that was for you. Then, wrap it up. Take a breather, and clear the energy. You can put on music, go for a walk, wiggle your arms and legs, jump up and down, cry, laugh, hug, high-five, beat a drum or play an instrument, stare out the window for a while, whatever—as long as it gives you an intentional break to clear the energy. Make sure to have at least one Heart Time during your three-month incubator.

The Friendship Incubator
Example agenda

Week 1: Cook dinner (or order takeout) at one of your houses.

Week 2: Go for a walk at a nearby park or check out a show at a local venue.

Week 3: Attend a meetup, museum, or class together.

Week 4: Hang out after work at one of your houses. Have Heart Time #1.

Week 5: Go for a walk in one or both of your neighborhoods.

Week 6: Arrange a small group outing with 2-3 additional people; Branch out when you select the activity: go to a show, lecture, class, nature setting, or volunteer activity together.

Week 7: Heart Time #2

Week 8: Happy hour or board game night

Week 9: Go for a mini-road trip to a nearby town. Eat pancakes at a diner. Ask the server to take your picture.

Week 10: Hang out at the other one of your houses. Make no plans. Just get together.

Week 11: Complete a task that you each need help with.

Week 12: Celebrate any way you like! And keep going any way that works for you both.

The Friendship Incubator makes use of all four Seeds of Connection by increasing your proximity, boosting your frequency, deepening your commitment, and developing your compatibility. It also gives you the same primary benefits as The QQ10 Method, but with much greater depth:

Momentum

One of the primary outcomes of this experiment is making friendship a regular part of your life. It's easier when you have built-in momentum keeping the ball rolling.

Continuity

The conversation just keeps going. One of the things people say they love about their bosom buddies is that "we can pick up where we left off." Keep that conduit open.

Authenticity

This experiment includes intentional challenges to invoke vulnerability. Be yourself and get to know each other for who you really are.

Familiarity

By the time you're done with this experiment, you'll have tried new things together, hung out at each other's houses, and had a memorable adventure together. This will make you more familiar and close with each other than you'd ever get from doing twice-a-year mimosa brunches or making small talk while watching the game at the local sports bar. You might even feel like you've got the beginning of a lifelong friendship.

In addition to the joy this experiment ought to bring, you can rest assured that a multitude of cognitive, behavioral, and social scientists are all cheering for you and betting on your success. According to them, you're bound to win.

MAKING IT REAL

In the spring of 2017, I was headed to my grandmother's funeral when I missed a connecting flight between Charlotte and Orlando. When the gate agent booked my replacement flight, I got upgraded to first class for the first time in my life. It was a short flight, only a couple hours, but I was still curious to see how flying first class would be different than flying in economy.

As I sat sipping a glass—a real glass—of orange juice, a middle-aged businessman dressed in crisp khakis and a navy polo sat down next to me. We'll call him Randall. After the plane took off, Randall and I began the customary single-serving friend conversation, starting with chit-chat about what cities we lived in. I told him why I was passing through, and he said he'd lived in Orlando for a decade and a half. I wondered whether I could ask him a personal question. He said he was game.

I asked him what his experience of friendship was like after living in his current city for fifteen years. I assumed that he would have a strong circle of friends and community, in contrast to the anemic one I had in the Bay Area where I'd only been living for a couple years.

"I don't really have any friends in my city," he said right off the bat.[1] "It sounds bad but those are the facts. I work outside of the town I live in, so I'm gone from Monday through Friday, almost every week. On the weekends when I get back, I'm only with my wife and family. The friends I do have are from the past, like people from college or my fraternity. The few people who I do know in town are more like acquaintances, and I met them either through church or socially. If I really wanted to hang out with somebody spontaneously, just to grab a beer and spend some time, I would have no one to call."

He went on to describe how, despite having the material resources to afford a beautiful house on five acres with a game room and a tennis court, he hasn't thrown a single successful party in the three years he's lived there. He shrugged with helpless disappointment as he reflected on the lost time and missed opportunities. "To make a party or get-together happen requires so much coordination and scheduling to get people to come over. And then even after sending out the invitations and buying all the food for a twenty-person BBQ, probably only two or three people would actually show up, even though a much larger number of people would have RSVP'd yes."

Randall contrasted his friendship experience to that of his grandfather's. "When I was a little boy, my granddad had a lot of friends in the area who he would regularly spend time with. There were about five of his friends within a 5-minute walk to his house. And he had another group of five friends who lived about 20 minutes away, but both groups of friends were connected to each other as a larger friend group. I remember seeing my granddad connect with my godfather and so many other friends in a real simple continuous way, from day to day, constantly." Randall said that the only people he's friendly with who he sees on a regular basis are his barber and the guys at the barbershop on weekends.

"I never really thought about this topic before," he continued. "It sounds sad to say, but honestly, if I died, aside from my family, I don't know who would come to my funeral. And I don't really know what to do about that. For example, my wife and I met another couple that we connected with at church, but to visit them is a 90-minute round trip, so we rarely see them. They live so far away. And on the rare occasion that we do get together with them, it's just for catching up, which is not the same thing as actually knowing each other."

One of the more hopeful things Randall said was that he's been actively trying to work his way down the ladder professionally so he can have more time to do other things in his life, including having friends. A successful career gave him a lot, but what he gave up in exchange for it cost more than he's willing to pay.

Where I'm at Now

It's just as hard to make friends today as it was six years ago when I moved to the Bay Area. The environment has stayed relatively the same—minus all the friends who've moved away. I've had some seriously disappointing and upsetting experiences with friendship, and some incredibly inspiring and motivating ones. It's been hard trying to make deep, long-lasting friendships in a place where it seems uniquely challenging to do so.

I got some surprising catharsis when I read the book *Who's Your City* by Dr. Richard Florida. In it, I learned that social scientists have verified that San Francisco really is a place where it's especially hard to make friends.[2] Dr. Florida and a team of psychologists and analysts crunched through enormous datasets to figure out the personalities of different cities and regions in the United States. Their findings confirm that there is a high concentration of highly-motivated people here who value ambition, creativity, independence, and who seek innovative experiences. On the flip side, there's also a low concentration of people here who value extroversion, duty, agreeableness, conscientiousness, social capital, and community ties. This blend of characteristics is common among large, creative cities that frequently give rise to innovative ideas. Sounds familiar. I don't expect this to change any time soon.

But I've changed. I've adjusted the way I respond to, and deal with, this problem. And with that, my whole situation has changed. I've tried many of the strategies on these pages and succeeded at achieving a more fulfilling depth in my friendships near and far. My main problem now is ensuring that I set aside time to see the recurring friends in my life as much as we want to see each other.

Getting to this place was not easy. There were some hard times when I wanted to throw in the towel, when I wondered if my strategy for friendship was all wrong. *"Maybe I shouldn't want to make close friends or best friends here,"* I thought. *"This environment seems to only support the formation of acquaintances (tons of them), "light" friends, and work friends. Maybe I should just worry less and invest in making the type of friendship that this place is uniquely adept at providing: the loose tie."*

Many times, I felt a lot like Nina, figuring that it'd be easier to just focus on the existing friendships I have with people who live far away. There's nothing wrong with that. In the first three seconds of a phone call or our rare face-to-face visits we are immediately dropped into the reassuring, warm arms of kinship. I wondered if I should just give my long-distance friends all of my attention. A lot of people choose this strategy.

The BBC podcast *The Why Factor* featured two episodes in 2018 about friendship.[3] In one episode, a woman they interviewed named Kate talked about how she keeps in touch with her three best friends that she met in college in Australia. Since graduating, they have all scattered across the globe: to London, Melbourne, L.A., and New York. They keep in touch with each other daily via an ongoing group chat.

"I've learned to conduct my best friendships over Whatsapp. It means I get to carry them around in my pocket all day long,"[3] she said. The women in her friend group message each other about the trivial details of their days and the big things in their lives. It didn't seem to bother her at all that her friends were hundreds or thousands of miles away. They couldn't go to a movie or dinner together, but she was in daily contact with all of them.

There were times when I stumbled on friendship speed-bumps locally, and I'd wonder if a globally dispersed friendship map is something I just needed to get used to. Relax locally, friend globally? Hmm. I don't think that's enough for me because I place such a high value on in-person friendships. While I don't want to let go of the beautiful friendships I have with wonderful people who now live far away, my ultimate goal is that no matter where I live, I'll be able to have kinship-level friendships and experiences of deep belonging, face to face too. I'm stubborn about this. I fully ascribe to the African proverb, "Home is not where we live. Home is where we belong." It's relatively easy to adopt a new address, but finding a new sense of belonging in adulthood can be considerably harder. I was determined to make it work, to prove, even if to no one but myself, that it's possible.

In the end, I've decided to focus on a small handful of local friendships that will ideally prove to be deep and long-lasting. I'm fertilizing my most promising friendships with as much dedicated time and attention that I can. Having spent the last few years immersed in this topic, I've studied what it takes to make a friendship take root, grow healthily, and survive the obstacles that life and interpersonal complications often throw in the way. Incorporating these practices into my life has helped me immensely. I offer them to you humbly with the highest intentions. I hope you are wildly successful.

Friendship is about more than fun or good feelings. Friends are the people who voluntarily love and care about you even when they're not obligated to by blood or familial expectations. And vice versa—you offer that care and love back to them. You don't need a ton of friends. Research validates what a lot of us already know to be true in practice: our satisfaction with our friendships is a better predictor of life satisfaction than the number of friends we have.[4]

While a good portion of this book contains advice for making friends, the thing to remember is that if we do a crap job of maintaining those friendships, then it doesn't matter how many friends we make. If our friendships are low quality, we'll be unsatisfied, and many of them will fizzle out and fade away. Then we have to start over.

Remember that the effort you put into any relationship, be it platonic, romantic, or familial, is an investment. Not all investments pay off, but for the ones that do, the payoff is sweet.

Taylor in Sydney sees the time-intensive work of cultivating friendships as a gift to her future self. "Cultivating friendships requires a lot of effort, energy, and time. You have to be willing to put yourself out there and expend that emotional energy because you're investing in your future happiness. And it goes both ways. Your friends are investing in you, hoping that you'll be a friend to them, and then you return the favor as much as possible."

Your Turn

If you've been having a hard time making new friends and maintaining existing friendships, please don't feel ashamed or embarrassed about it. Talk to other people about it. Statistically, there's a 50/50 chance that any person you talk to will feel the same way.[5] When I encountered this problem, I was embarrassed to talk about it at first, but once I did, I found that things quickly started getting better.

In the beginning, I didn't know how to mention this topic or bring it up. Once I started working on this book, voilà, I had my opening. By telling people that I was working on a book about friendship, I could talk about the issues that led me to this project. Interestingly, I found that by having open conversations about the challenges I faced, my friendships, even with new people, started getting better quicker. There are people everywhere who are craving this conversation.

Obviously, not everyone can say they're working on a book about friendship, but you *can* say that you recently finished reading a book about friendship. Boom, there's your opening. If it's something you really want to talk about, practice asking people questions like, "What was it like making friends when you moved here?" or "Can I ask you a question—what's your experience of friendship like these days?" If you've been unsatisfied with your own journey through adult friendship, open up about it. Or even better, start a discussion group using this book to kickstart your conversations. I've included helpful guides at the back of this book for exactly this purpose, along with hundreds of conversation starters that I've written and collected over the last five years. Take action and make the invitation.

You are now equipped with tools and strategies to help you figure out what needs attention in your own friendship garden. Use them to clarify your challenges, your priorities, and the best set of solutions for you to overcome them. If you want, be creative and make up your own ideas to add to your list of tools. Experiment. Be bold. Be honest. Be brave. Make choices that will allow you to show up as the best friend you can absolutely be. By being the kind of friend you wish you had, you invite others to do the same, too.

Solving the friendship problem comes down to one basic thing. Simply put: we should get together. Whenever we can, wherever we can, in whatever format makes it possible. We should get together when it's convenient, and when it's not. We should change the way we think about time in order to make it happen. We should get together in new ways: openly, unguardedly, honestly, curiously, empathetically, vulnerably, creatively. We should get together with our neighbors. We should get together at home and outside the home, whether it's scheduled or spontaneous, but especially when we can do it calmly, gently, with ease and spaciousness.

We should get together in public, and we should get together in private. We should get together in nature. We should get together in new places, and in the places where we feel cozy and relaxed. We should get together wherever we can speak about what's on our minds and in our hearts. We should make the most of it when we do get together, by trading in the small talk for real talk. We should get together when we say we will. We should get together like it really matters. Because it does.

After Friendship: Cultivate Community

When you're ready to move beyond individual friendship cultivation, turn your imagination towards creating a thriving community that manifests all the same positive qualities of healthy friendships. Recruit your friends to join you. I'd love to hear how it goes.

www.weshouldgettogether.com

BOOK CLUB DISCUSSION GUIDE

The best way to practice the lessons in this book is to apply them in real life in your friendships with other people. Beyond that, another great way to integrate the lessons is to talk about your reflections on them with your book clubs, meetups, and discussion groups. Here are a few questions to get you started. Get more ideas and resources at weshouldgettogether.com.

General Questions

What's your experience of friendship like these days—both in person and long distance?

How do you intentionally cultivate and care for your friendships? What's working or not working?

What friendship challenges are you facing?

Hydroponic Friendship

Which of the Seeds of Connection feel like the biggest priority to you?

Which feel like the hardest to access or cultivate?

Hypermobility & Belonging

How long do you plan to live in your current city?

How has moving, or staying put, affected your experience of friendship?

If you were to lose access to all of your long-distance friends tonight, how would your in-town friendships be affected if at all?

Busyness & Spaciousness

How does busyness or spaciousness show up in your life?

Do you ever catch yourself using busyness as a crutch? If so, what for?

Which do you value more: your achievements or your wellbeing? Your accomplishments or your relationships? How does your schedule reflect your priorities and values?

Even if nothing else changed in your schedule, what would it mean for you to stop saying you were busy? What would you say instead? What would it mean if you made different choices that resulted in you feeling less busy?

How often do you make time for connecting with friends, and why?

Are you following any arbitrary rules about how and when you can see or talk to your friends?

What's one way that you could spend time with a friend(s) that you haven't done in the past and would like to?

Partnership & Family

How does being in a relationship (or not) affect your experience of friendship?

How does having children (or not) affect your experience of friendship?

What's one thing you can do differently, or that you can ask a friend to do differently, to support your shared friendship?

Intimacy & Depth

Is there something in your life you need help with that you're not reaching out and asking for help with?

Is there a friend that you need to break up with? How will you go about that?

What is one way that you can be a better friend to others?

What's your plan for ensuring you have access to robust friendship and community as you get older?

Acknowledgments

Writing a book is a lot of work, and I couldn't have done it without the help of many people along the way.

First, I'd like to thank everyone who opened up and shared their stories with me over the last several years. Many of you appear on these pages. There are many more people whose stories aren't here in ink, but who are absolutely here in heart. Thank you for opening up to me about your experiences—both heartwarming and heart-wrenching. This book would be nothing without you.

I'd also like to thank everyone who has ever attended *Better than Small Talk*. You helped me continue to believe that it's possible to create better communities by having the courage to get together in new ways. My deep belief in the power of well-timed, thoughtful, and expertly facilitated questions comes from The Power of Hope/Partners for Youth Empowerment who were instrumental in shaping who I am and how I navigate the world. Thank you to Peggy Taylor and Charlie Murphy (RIP) for creating a worldwide creative community and for teaching me so much about how to convene groups with intention and create community from scratch. To everyone I've befriended as part of POH/PYE, you're absolutely here too, and I'm immensely grateful to have you in my life.

Many thanks to Jack Shriner, Julia Nguyen, and Laura Parker for sharing your expertise and perspectives on how people can cultivate stronger mental health and friendship, and for everything you do to help others live fuller and healthier lives. Thanks also to Dr. Jeffrey Hall at the Relationships and Technology Lab at the University of Kansas. Your research is endlessly fascinating to me and I'm grateful for all that you do to help people better understand how to get more out of their connections with others.

Big thanks to Jessica Hadari and the entire Femtalks community for your positivity, exuberance, and encouragement. I am deeply grateful for the way you create a safe container for women to grow and support each other in sharing our gifts with the world.

Deep gratitude to Shannon Weber, Beth Barany, Cristina Orbe, and Linda Flavin for your enthusiasm, wisdom, and advice on the many ways I could get this book and this message into the world.

Huge thanks to Sarah Park, to my Oakland writers circle (Steve, Rebecca, Susie, Sasha, Leslie, Abigail), and to my beta readers (Jen, Shannon, Steve, Tony, Spark, Sophie, Mekael.) Thank you for reading my embarassingly rough drafts and for giving me advice with the utmost kindness about how I could polish them up. You have truly helped me become a better writer and a better person.

A deep bow of gratitude also goes to Majo Molfino for your encouragement and support, and for introducing me to Katie.

Tremendous thanks to all the friends and allies who offered me their support as I worked to make this book a reality: the friends near and far, Balthazar and Rae (you know who you are), Annie, my dear brother Mekael, and my beloved Jen. Your dedication, curiosity, patience, and love are among my greatest treasures.

Last but certainly not least, I extend the deepest gratitude to my editor Katie Salisbury for your expert guidance, advice, questions, recommendations, and skillful hand. Your masterful support helped me get from a draft that was trying to be a book, to a finished version that I'm truly proud of.

Apologies to anyone I may have left out, and for any errors in this book, which are fully my own.

Find Your Feelings

Understanding your feelings is key to navigating them successfully and communicating them to others. This single succinct chart is one of my favorite resources for helping with that process.

	Happy	Caring	Confident	High/Low Energy	Guilt or Shame	Apathetic	Fearful	Sad	Angry	Uncertain
Mild *A little* *A little bit* *Slightly* *Mildly*	Glad Grateful Pleased Content Satisfied	Appreciative Friendly Interested in Intrigued by Tender Understanding Warmly toward	Committed Competent Dedicated Determined Focused	Calm Chill Laid back Open Serene	Bashful Chagrined Embarrassed Hesitant Reluctant Sheepish	Disinterested Dull Flat	Cautious On edge Shy Tense Tentative Timid Uncomfortable Uneasy	Disappointed Down Glum In a funk Lonely Low Somber Subdued Unhappy	Annoyed Bugged Frustrated Grouchy Impatient Irritated Miffed Raw Sullen	Bothered Confused Distracted Startled Surprised Undecided Unsettled Unsure
Medium	Cheerful Delighted In high spirits Jovial Light-hearted Merry Optimistic Playful	Admiring Affectionate Close to Compassionate Concern for Empathetic Loving Trusting Warm-hearted	Brave Hopeful Optimistic Proud Receptive Resilient	Awake Eager Excited Lazy Relaxed Tired Worn out	Apologetic Contrite Crummy Exposed Guilty Regretful Remorseful Sorry	Aloof Bored Vacant Indifferent Unaffected	Afraid Alarmed Anxious Apprehensive Frightened Worried Nervous Scared	Dejected Disconnected Discouraged Distressed Gloomy Hurt Insignificant Melancholy Upset	Aggravated Agitated Defensive Dismayed Exasperated Indignant Mad Pissed off Resentful	Bewildered Blurry Foggy Lost Misunderstood Perplexed Puzzled Stuck
Strong *Extremely* *Really* *Very* *Super*	Amazed Ecstatic Elated Euphoric Exhilarated Overjoyed Thrilled	Adoring Crazy about Devoted Enamored Engrossed Fascinated Passionate Protective over Wild about Zealous	Inspired Daring Brash Bold	Energetic Enthusiastic Exhausted Fatigued Pumped up Weary	Ashamed Delinquent Disgraced Horrible Humiliated Inept Mortified Useless Worthless	—	Distressed Horrified Intimidated Panicked Paralyzed Petrified Shocked Terrified	Awful Crushed Depressed Desolate Despondent Grieved Hopeless Miserable	Bitter Disgusted Enraged Furious Irate Outraged Vengeful Vindictive	Baffled Confounded Overwhelmed Powerless Rattled Shocked Stumped Taken aback

Emotions Chart created by and provided courtesy of Anamaria Nino-Murcia and Michael Terrell, Founders of Fort Light, and Gary Dexter; Lecturer at the Stanford Graduate School of Business. For more information, see fortlight.com and gsb.stanford.edu

Better than Small Talk
The Conversation Starters

Where in your life would you like to have better conversations? Holidays, hikes, camping, dinner parties, meetings, team-building activities, flights, road trips? Anywhere you gather is a good place for a great conversation. Since 2015, the *Better than Small Talk* conversation-starters have been helping people form and strengthen friendships, build community, and have better conversations. Friends, families, coworkers, classmates and strangers have developed more authentic connections with each other and transformed the way they relate, understand each other, and see the world. With these conversation starters in your bag, you'll always have plenty of fabulous ideas to get a really wonderful conversation going. They will help you move past small talk and build better connections with the people around you. All it takes is the courage to ask a new question.

Reflection

- Did you ever try to get away with anything when you were a kid?
- Do you ever feel lonely? If so, when?
- How have you changed as a person since you were 16?
- Do you ever think about your friends from high school? If so, when do they cross your mind?
- Has a book ever changed your life? If yes, what book was it and how did it affect you?
- When was the last time you danced in public?
- If you don't look at your phone for a few hours, how do you feel? (Sleeping doesn't count.)
- Share a memory about a place you've been to outside of this country. If you haven't travelled yet, where would you want to go?
- What's a memory that you really love?
- What's the last thing that you took a photo of and why?
- What have you been thinking about a lot lately?
- What do you do within the first 15 minutes of being awake?
- What's the weirdest job you've ever had?
- Do remember your dreams? Do you think dreams serve any purpose for you?
- When's the last time you painted something?
- Tell a story about a time when you felt embarrassed.
- What was your first job?
- What's a music memory that you have?
- What's something you were nervous to try eating but really liked?
- What's something you haven't eaten in a really long time that you'd like to have again?

- Tell a short story about a time when your first impression was totally wrong.
- What were three songs that you loved as a teenager?
- How do you normally spend Saturday morning?
- Has any band or musician had a significant impact on your life?
- What's something that worked out really well lately?
- What's a time when you were really scared?
- What's a time when you felt full of joy and happiness?
- Has a piece of art (music, art, film) ever brought you to tears?
- Tell a story about a time when you were not completely honest.
- Have you ever surprised yourself?
- Describe the first time you tasted alcohol.
- What's one of the hardest things you've done, that you're glad you did?
- What was a time during the last year when you felt the most alive?
- What's something that's really concerned you lately?
- How much do you know about what was happening in the world the year you were born?
- Have your values ever stopped you from doing something you wanted to do?
- Have you ever been naked in a public place?
- If you could relive any one year of your life, which would you pick and why?
- Describe a time when you felt really connected to or amazed by nature.
- What's a risk you took that worked out well?
- What's a hard decision you've had to make recently?
- Talk about the first time you remember leaving your hometown.
- Do you think you've ever made a bad decision? If so, what was it?

- What sweets did you love as a child?
- Which do you think is more important to have: a sense of purpose or a feeling of belonging?
- What are some of your favorite comfort foods?
- When you were a child, did elders in your life ever say certain sayings or proverbs about life? If so, what are one or two that you remember?
- What was a low point during this year for you? How did you handle it or move past it?
- Have you ever laughed until you cried? What do you think makes this kind of funny different from regular kinds of funny?
- Who's a person you knew in your childhood that you still think about sometimes?
- What were some of your favorite books or stories from when you were a kid?
- If you could change one thing about today, what would it be?
- What are two things you're grateful for that happened in the last year?
- As you've gotten older, have you outgrown any previously-held beliefs?
- Have you ever spoken in front of a large group of people? If yes, what did you learn from the experience?
- What are some places that you feel connected to?
- Have you ever regretted a purchase? Had something turn out to be a total waste of money?
- Have you ever been really excited to buy something? If yes, what was it?
- How do you feel about holidays?

Imagination

- If you could wake up tomorrow with two new talents or abilities, what would they be?
- What's the scariest thing you would try if you were guaranteed to survive unscathed?
- What's something about the natural world that fascinates you?
- If you had to go live in another country for the rest of your life, where would you pick and why?
- If you could press a button and suddenly know how to speak every language in the world OR play every instrument in the world, which would you pick?
- If you had to give up dancing or listening to live music forever, which would you pick and why?
- If you had to pick one of your senses to give up tomorrow, which would you pick, and what about it would you miss the most?
- If you had the power to control your dreams at night, would you?
- Do you think there is life anywhere else in the universe? If yes, what do you think it's like?
- Where does creativity come from?
- Would you rather have the ability to speak every verbal language in the world, or to communicate telepathically?
- If you could create a second Earth for humans to populate, how would you make it different from this one?
- If you were going to become famous next year for something, what would you want to be famous for?
- Is there anything that you've done that you wish more people knew about?

- If you could artificially enhance your brain to stay faster and sharper than the average human brain, would you? This ability would persist until you die.
- If you couldn't have a passport, would you be ok with never going to another country again, or would you try to go anyway?
- Would you rather live a life of great meaning even if it came with experiences of great sadness, or would you rather life a completely happy life that lacked any real depth?
- If you could spend one week in any future year of your choosing, which would you pick and what would you want to do?
- If you had to give up talking or touch, which would you pick and why?
- If you could choose to perpetually feel 25% less anger, anxiety, or frustration than your average level, which would you pick and why?
- If you could perpetually feel 25% more gratitude, curiosity or silliness than your average level, which would you pick and why?
- What's a possibility that you dream of making real?
- What do you think your life would be like right now if you were living in one of the cities that interests you but that you've never been to?
- Can you think of ten ways to prepare and eat bananas?
- Which do you think are better, the years behind you or the ones yet to come?
- What do you think was happening in your exact location 100 years ago?
- What's something that you think would be fun to try doing?
- Do you think animals have conscious intentional thoughts?
- What do you think the world will be like in 200 years?

- How do you think you would change if you didn't watch any movies or read any books for the next year?
- If you found out today that you would get sudden and extreme dementia on your 80th birthday, how would that change your path, if at all?
- Do you think that what we call reality is actually real?
- Describe your dream house
- Describe your ideal neighborhood.
- Do you think there is anything positive about your brain forgetting things?
- What's one word you want to define the next year of your life?
- If you knew you would be guaranteed success, what is something you would try doing?
- If you woke up tomorrow with the ability to speak every language on Earth, how would it change your life if at all?
- If you could change one decision you've made, what would it be?
- What kinds of things do you wonder about?
- What would the Wikipedia article about you say happened in the next ten years of your life?
- Do you think life was better for humans before we started forming cities?
- Tell the person across from you three jobs you could imagine them doing well.
- Do you think that human existence has been a good thing for the universe?
- If you won the lottery, how do you think your life would change?
- If you had to give up one of the following forever, which would you choose and why: plumbing, motorized vehicles, or electricity

- If you had to eat dinner every night with a new stranger, what sort of conversations would you like to have?
- Imagine that you've just reached the top of the bestseller list for a book you've written. What is the book about?
- Would you rather walk on the moon, or explore the depths of the ocean?
- If you could go back in time to spend a week with one of your great-grandparents, which would you pick and why?
- How do you think your life would change if you devoted yourself to minimalism for the next ten years?
- What would be your ideal way to spend a month of free time?
- If you were going to be interviewed on a national media program, what would you want to talk about?
- If you were going to write the lyrics to a song that you knew would become #1 on the charts, what would the topic of the song be?
- What do you think would happen if, for one week only, people were incapable of lying and everyone told the complete truth?

Identity

- Do you practice self-care? If yes, what are some examples of self-care that really nourish you?
- Do you ever feel happy, content, or peaceful? If yes, when do you feel those emotions?
- If you didn't have to work to live comfortably, what would you do with your unlimited free time?
- How do you want to be remembered when your life is over?
- What do you do with your selfies?
- Before it was possible to take pictures with a phone, when did you take self portraits?
- In what ways are you a creative person?
- What are some things that annoy the crap out of you?
- Have you ever volunteered before? If yes, what was your most recent volunteer role?
- How do you feel when you're in a really big crowd?
- What were you like as a 16 year old? How are you similar to that child, and how are you different?
- In what ways are you weird?
- When did you first realize that you have a sense of humor?
- Do you still get excited? If no, why do you think you don't get excited anymore? If yes, what kinds of things elicit your excitement?
- What are two things you are really, really good at?
- If you could only do one kind of exercise for the rest of your life, what would it be?
- How comfortable are you with being the center of attention?

- What's something you think about that other people seem to never think about?
- Are you afraid of vulnerability?
- If you were going to wake up tomorrow as another race or ethnicity than your own, which would you pick and why?
- What are two things you're afraid of, and what's something you can do to minimize those fears?
- What are three things that are true about you that someone can't tell by looking at you?
- When do you feel most anxious? When do you feel most calm?
- Do you consider yourself to be creative? Why or why not?
- Would you ever call yourself an artist? Why or why not?
- Are there any personality traits or qualities that you wish you had more of?
- As you get older, are you getting more cynical or more optimistic?
- Have you ever done something kind for someone else and kept it a secret?
- When do you know that it's time to quit something?
- Have you ever done something in front of a crowd that you were nervous to do? If yes, what was it?
- How old do you want to live to be?
- What are some of the qualities of people you admire?
- What advice would your 80-year-old self give you today?
- What were you like as a 5-year-old? How are you similar to that child, and how are you different?
- Where do you feel most at home?
- Describe who you are without using your name, job, nationality, or birthplace.

- If you could snap your fingers and get rid of one of your fears immediately, which would you pick and why?
- What is a big lesson you've learned in your life and how did you learn it?
- What kinds of things do you find funny?
- Do you have any core values that guide your life and how you live it?
- What are two things you're really bad at?
- What's your earliest memory?
- Would you rather be thought of as very charismatic or very reliable?
- Are you more introverted or extroverted? What are the reasons for your answer?
- What's a lesson that has stuck with you since childhood?
- Has anything happened this year that's changed you in a significant way?
- What do you think about life coaching?
- If you could have any superpower, what would it be?
- What kinds of stories do you find yourself continually drawn to?
- What are three of your best qualities?
- Is it easy or difficult to change your behaviors? Do you think you can change who you are at your core?
- What's one thing you would change about yourself?
- What's a capacity or strength you want to develop by this time next year?
- What are some of the qualities of people you dislike?
- Have you ever had a mentor or been a mentee? If yes, what was the experience like?

Relationships

- Would you rather your parents chose your friends or your spouse?
- What do you think "falling in love" really is?
- How do you think your experience of friendship would change if you couldn't use social media anymore?
- Do you think it's possible to feel love for someone you've only ever talked to online?
- What public displays of affection do you think are appropriate?
- Would you hug a stranger? Why or why not?
- If you could pick three people to live in your city, who would you pick and why?
- What do you do when you have a crush on someone?
- If you could pick any two people to have as next door neighbors, who would you pick and why?
- Do you know your neighbors, and does it matter to you to know your neighbors?
- What qualities make you a really good partner?
- Have you ever shared something really personal with someone you didn't know very well?
- Have you ever been in love? If yes, how did you know you were in love?
- Do you believe that there is something good in everyone?
- Do you miss anyone who is far away? If yes, who is it and why do you miss them so much?
- What is a parent's job?
- Do you have a sense of community in your life? What's your experience of community like these days?

- Have you ever had an experience of really feeling like you were part of a team? What was it like?
- Have you ever grown apart from a friend? If yes, how did you handle it?
- If you were hospitalized for a week, who do you think would come to visit you?
- If you were going to trade lives with any of your family members, who would you pick and why?
- What's a question you ask other people that you wish other people would ask you?
- How do you define love?
- What are the qualities of a real, true, good friend?
- Do you have any enemies?
- If you could change anything about your family, what would it be?
- Who's someone you have a hard time loving but you keep trying anyway?
- What do you think about online dating apps?
- Do you think you could be happy in an arranged marriage?
- Do you have as many friends as you want?
- What do you think is the best way to deal with bullies?
- What do you think about holidays like Mothers Day, Fathers Day, and Valentines Day?
- If you were going to spend next week living with any friend, who would you pick and why?
- What makes it difficult for people to open up and be genuine with each other?
- Did you have any relationship with your grandparents or great grandparents?

- Describe your ideal romantic partner.
- If you had to spend the rest of your life sharing a home with one person that you do not currently live with, who would you pick and why?
- What's a compliment you could give to the person you're talking to right now?
- Have you ever done something kind for a stranger? If yes, what was it?
- What's something you apologized for recently, and why were you sorry?
- "Describe an apology that you've received from someone else and how their apology made you feel."
- Has anyone ever asked you to change one of your behaviors? If yes, what was it and how did that go?
- Do you think it's important to be friends outside of work with your coworkers?
- Do you think small talk is an effective way to get to know people?
- What's one question that you think would make a great addition to the regular set of small talk questions?
- What are the characteristics of friendships in which you feel really connected to the other person?
- Would you rather spend the rest of your life unpartnered or in an unfulfilling partnership?
- When interacting with others, do you think you're too tough or too soft?
- Who is an acquaintance that you think you'd really like to be better friends with?
- Do you believe in love at first sight?

- What's something valuable you learned from an ex?
- Are you still close to the people you were friends with in high school?
- Has a teacher ever made a lasting impact on your life? If yes, how?
- If you're in a relationship, what's one thing you love about your partner and one thing you would change?
- If you were hospitalized for a week, who do you think would come to visit you?

Learning

- Is there anything you wish that you'd had a chance to learn as a child or teenager?
- Do you actively seek out opportunities to learn new things?
- If you had to be a teacher for the rest of your life, what would you teach?
- Has a teacher ever inspired you?
- Should students have a chance to grade their teachers? If yes, what should happen to teachers based on the grades they get?
- What's a time you were really out of your comfort zone, and what did you learn from the experience?
- What's something that you've taught to someone else?
- Do you think it's possible for someone to live a well-informed, educated life if they never read books?
- If you had to give up reading books or social media forever, which would you choose?

- Do you have any tricks to making life better?
- What's a book that you think everyone should read?
- If you were going to go to university for 4 years starting tomorrow, what would you want to study the most?
- What have you learned from your experiences of sadness and joy?
- Are there any subjects that you wish you knew more about?
- What was your favorite subject in school and why?
- If you could only consume media (books, movies, tv, social media, etc) about one topic for the rest of your life, what topic would you pick and why?
- What are two valuable things you've learned this year?
- If you could only keep 3 books in your home for the rest of your life, which books would you choose?
- What was the last class you took and how did you feel about it?
- If you could never read/listen to/or watch the news again, who is the one person you would trust to keep you informed?
- If you could wake up tomorrow as the world's foremost expert about any topic, what would you pick and why?
- If you were going to devote yourself to any entrepreneurial goal for the next ten years, what would it be?
- If you had to spend one hour a day studying a topic or practicing a skill, what would you pick and why?
- What's something you've learned from observing a friend's life?
- Who or what do you turn to when you need advice or perspective?
- What's an adult life skill that you wish you were better at?
- What do you think about the way that children are educated in this country?
- Are you satisfied with the number of languages that you know?

- Do you think everything you learned in school was true? Why or why not?
- Tell a short story about a time you doubted your abilities and how you handled it.
- What's the longest amount of time you've been silent and what did you learn from that experience?
- Describe an ideal educational environment for young children.
- Describe an ideal educational environment for teenagers.
- Describe an ideal educational environment for adults.
- What's the longest amount of time you've been silent?
- If you were going to give a speech to all the teenagers in this country, what would you talk about?
- Did you learn anything in school that has proven to be useless knowledge?
- What learning styles do you identify with most:

  Visual / Spatial

  Aural / Auditory-Musical

  Verbal / Linguistic

  Physical / Kinesthetic

  Logical / Mathematical

  Social / Interpersonal

  Solitary / Intrapersonal

- Have you ever quit learning something because it was too hard? If so, what was it?
- Would you rather become an expert in the topics you're already well-versed in, or trade everything you know for set of new topics that you'd be equally well-versed in?
- Do you think that the schools you went to cared about the kids?

- What's a lesson that life keeps trying to teach you?
- What was one of the last things you researched about on the internet or in a book?
- What are two topics you know a lot about?
- Do you prefer being a student or a teacher?
- Is there any topic that you're glad you don't know about, because your ignorance about that topic gives you some positive benefit?
- What's something that you've put off learning about, that you intend to start learning about sometime soon?
- As you've gotten older, have you outgrown any previously-held beliefs?
- How do you intend to keep your brain functioning at a high level as you age?
- What's something that you know how to cook really well? How did you learn to make it?
- If you could improve your memory for any one type of information, what would you pick and why?
- Have you learned anything in the last year that shocked you?
- What's something that you think people would be surprised to learn about you?
- Do you have street smarts? If yes, how did you learn them?
- How well can you navigate your city without the use of maps or GPS?

Society

- Do you say hello and look people in the eye when you pass them on the street? Why or why not?
- Does using technology make you feel more connected or more disconnected?
- How important is it to keep up with world affairs?
- What do you think is the ultimate waste of money?
- How do you decide what parts of the news you'll pay attention to?
- How does the society you live in reflect your personal values? How does it not?
- What do you think are over-valued and under-valued in society?
- Would you rather live in a country with no ethnic diversity or no music?
- What do you like about small talk? What do you dislike about it?
- When's the last time you talked to a stranger about something that wasn't small talk?
- When you're at a party and feel kind of bored, what do you do?
- If you were going to be the leader of your country for the next five years, what would be your top priorities? (Try to focus on answering the question versus venting about the current political climate).
- If you could change anything about your neighborhood, what would you change?
- What are three things that you wish the people in your city would all start doing?
- What do you think is the biggest problem facing the planet in the future? What do you think is also our biggest hope or opportunity?
- Describe your ideal neighborhood.

- Do you think people are more connected or more isolated from each other than they were in the past?
- What do you think is overvalued in pop culture?
- What do you enjoy or appreciate from popular culture?
- What's one practice, habit, law, or rule you think our country should adopt from another country?
- If you could make one major problem in this country vanish forever, what would you pick and why?
- What is one thing that you think should be free for all people?
- Do you think the internet has made the world a better place?
- What would it take for you to give up using the internet forever?
- Which do you think is more important to have in a society: individual self-expression or group harmony?
- Do you think our society is smarter and kinder than it was twenty years ago? Fifty years ago?
- Describe what your ideal environment for growing old would look like.
- How do you show the world what you care about?
- Does it matter to you if your clothes are made in sweatshops overseas? Why or why not?
- How do you think elections would change if candidates weren't allowed to give speeches when they were running for office?
- What value, if any, do celebrities bring to society?
- What are three of your favorite things about the city you live in?
- Do you see more people expressing dissatisfaction or gratitude in your day to day life?
- What, if any, lies do you think are acceptable for people to tell each other?

- Do you feel free? Why or why not?
- If all your basic needs and spending money would be provided as long as you devoted your life to service, what cause would you pick and why?
- Do you think people in our society will ever be truly equal? If yes, what would it take to make that happen?
- Do you think that people should be required to give back to society in some way?
- How comfortable do you feel talking to a total stranger?
- Do you think social media has made the world better or worse?
- How would you describe the personality of your city: positive and negative?
- How a scale of 1-10 how grateful are you for the invention of the internet? Why did you choose your answer?
- What do you think are the qualities of a good leader?
- Do you think that pop music affects how people treat each other?
- Do you think that movies and TV shows make a meaningful contribution to society or not?
- What do you think is the difference between a first impression and a snap judgment? Or do you think these are the same thing?
- Do you think holidays are important for a society to have? Why or why not?
- Have you ever thrown a party and invited a bunch of your neighbors that you barely knew? Would you?
- What is one app or website that you can't live without? What's one that you wish would disappear forever?
- Imagine that you're in charge of coming up with an alternative to modern-day capitalism. What would it look like?

- Do you think that being exposed to movies, TV, apps and popular music is good for children? Why or why not?
- What are three headlines you would love to see on the front page of the newspaper?
- What's something you love about this country, and something you would change if you could?
- Do you prefer to be friends with your neighbors or not?
- If you were going to have a neighbor over for dinner, who would you pick and why?

Notes

Introduction

1. Zoya Gervis, "Why the Average American Hasn't Made a New Friend in 5 Years," *New York Post*, May 9, 2019, https://nypost.com/2019/05/09/why-the-average-american-hasnt-made-a-new-friend-in-5-years/

2. Vijeth Iyengar PhD., "Why Social Isolation Is Bad for Us as We Age (And What We Can Do to Combat It)," *Psychology Benefits Society*, July 10, 2018, https://psychologybenefits.org/2018/07/10/why-social-isolation-is-bad-for-us-as-we-age-and-what-we-can-do-to-combat-it/

3. Douglas Nemecek M.D., MBA. ,"Cigna U.S. Loneliness Index," *Cigna*, May 1, 2018, https://www.cigna.com/assets/docs/newsroom/loneliness-survey-2018-full-report.pdf

4. Administrator, "Social isolation, loneliness in older people pose health risks," *National Institute on Aging*, April 23, 2019, https://www.nia.nih.gov/news/social-isolation-loneliness-older-people-pose-health-risks

5. Jena McGregor, "This Former Surgeon General Says There's a 'Loneliness Epidemic' and Work Is Partly to Blame," *The Washington Post*, WP Company, October 4, 2017, https://www.washingtonpost.com/news/on-leadership/wp/2017/10/04/this-former-surgeon-general-says-theres-a-loneliness-epidemic-and-work-is-partly-to-blame/?utm_term=.dae8ea63c6cb

6. Roni Caryn Rabin, "Talk Deeply, Be Happy?" *The New York Times*, March 17, 2010, https://well.blogs.nytimes.com/2010/03/17/talk-deeply-be-happy/

How Friendship Got So Complicated

1. Wikipedia contributors, "Lean on Me (song)," *Wikipedia, The Free Encyclopedia*, https://en.wikipedia.org/w/index.php?title=Lean_on_Me_(song)&oldid=921933807

2. Yang Claire Yang, Courtney Boen, Karen Gerken, Ting Li, Kristen Schorpp, and Kathleen Mullan Harris. "Social Relationships and Physiological Determinants of Longevity across the Human Life Span." *Proceedings of the National Academy of Sciences* 113, no. 3 (2016): 578–83, accessed September 2018, https://doi.

org/10.1073/pnas.1511085112

3. Douglas Nemecek M.D., MBA. ,"Cigna U.S. Loneliness Index," *Cigna*, May 1, 2018, https://www.cigna.com/assets/docs/newsroom/loneliness-survey-2018-full-report.pdf

4. Erin Schumaker, "What A Surgeon General Learned From The Opioid Crisis Could Help Fight Loneliness." *HuffPost*, October 9, 2017, https://www.huffpost.com/entry/surgeon-general-vivek-murthy-loneliness-opioid_n_59db8529e4b07 2637c457d4e

5. Jane E. Brody, "Personal Health," *The New York Times*, April 6, 1983, https://www.nytimes.com/1983/04/06/garden/personal-health-079788.html

6. Katerina V.-A. Johnson and Robin I. M. Dunbar, "Pain Tolerance Predicts Human Social Network Size," Nature News. *Nature Publishing Group*, April 28, 2016, https://www.nature.com/articles/srep25267

7. Julianne Holt-Lunstad, Timothy B. Smith, and J. Bradley Layton, "Social Relationships and Mortality Risk: A Meta-Analytic Review," *PLoS Medicine* 7, no. 7 (2010), https://doi.org/10.1371/journal.pmed.1000316

8. Katherine Boydell, "Social Prescribing: Linking Patients with Non-Medical Support," InsightPlus, February 25, 2019, https://insightplus.mja.com.au/2019/7/social-prescribing-linking-patients-with-non-medical-support/

9. Michael Dixon, "How Social Prescribing Is Cutting the NHS Drugs Bill," The Guardian, *Guardian News and Media*, September 17, 2014, https://www.theguardian.com/healthcare-network/2014/sep/17/social-prescribing-cutting-nhs-drugs-bill

10. Christopher Ingraham, "Americans Say There's Not Much Appeal to Big-City Living. Why Do so Many of Us Live There?," The Washington Post, *WP Company*, December 19, 2018, https://www.washingtonpost.com/business/2018/12/18/americans-say-theres-not-much-appeal-big-city-living-why-do-so-many-us-live-there/

11. Sam Meredith, "Two-Thirds of Global Population Will Live in Cities by 2050, UN Says.," *CNBC*, May 17, 2018, https://www.cnbc.com/2018/05/17/two-thirds-of-global-population-will-live-in-cities-by-2050-un-says.html

12. Charles Montgomery, *Happy City: Transforming Our Lives through Urban Design*, 194–195, 278-279, (Toronto, Ontario: Anchor Canada, 2014), "Chapter 8: Mobilicities I: How Moving Feels and Why It Does Not Feel Better"; "Chapter 12: Retrofitting Sprawl."

13. Louis Wirth, "Urbanism as a Way of Life," *American Journal of Sociology 44*, no. 1 (Jul., 1938): 1-24, https://doi.org/10.1086/217913

Hydroponic Friendship

1. Jeffrey A. Hall PhD., "How Many Hours Does It Take to Make a Friend?," *Journal of Social and Personal Relationships* 36, no. 4 (2018): 1278–96, https://doi.org/10.1177/0265407518761225

2. Wikipedia contributors, "Hydroponics," *Wikipedia, The Free Encyclopedia*, https://en.wikipedia.org/w/index.php?title=Hydroponics&oldid=921929332, accessed March 2018

Seeds of Connection: Proximity

1. Wikipedia contributors, "Proximity principle," *Wikipedia, The Free Encyclopedia*, https://en.wikipedia.org/w/index.php?title=Proximity_principle&oldid=898364514, accessed August 2018

2. Richard L. Florida PhD., *Who's Your City? How the Creative Economy Is Making Where to Live the Most Important Decision of Your Life* (New York, NY: Basic Books, 2008), Chapter 5: "The Mobile and The Rooted", 87–87.

3. Melissa Dahl, "A Third of Americans Have Never Met Their Neighbors," *The Cut*, August 24, 2015, https://www.thecut.com/2015/08/third-of-americans-dont-know-their-neighbors.html

Seeds of Connection: Frequency

1. Jeffrey A. Hall PhD., "How Many Hours Does It Take to Make a Friend?" *Journal of Social and Personal Relationships*, vol. 36, no. 4, 2018, pp. 1278–1296., doi:10.1177/0265407518761225

2. Angelica (not her real name) in discussion with the author, December 2018.

3. Susie Neilson, "In Old Age, Friends Might Matter Even More Than Family," *The Cut*, June 16, 2017, https://www.thecut.com/2017/06/in-old-age-friends-might-matter-even-more-than-family.html

4. Survey by the author, www.adultfriendshipsurvey.com

Seeds of Connection: Compatibility

1. "Compatibility," Dictionary.com. Dictionary.com, n.d. https://www.dictionary.com/browse/compatibility?s=t, accessed June 2018

2. Survey by the author, www.adultfriendshipsurvey.com

3. Edelman and Publicis, "Heineken® - USA." Heineken® - USA, 2017, https://www.heineken.com/gb/videos/worlds-apart.

4. https://www.hifromtheotherside.com/

Seeds of Connection: Commitment

1. Debra L. Oswald, Eddie M. Clark, and Cheryl M. Kelly. "Friendship Maintenance: An Analysis of Individual and Dyad Behaviors." *Journal of Social and Clinical Psychology* 23, no. 3 (2004): 413–41, https://doi.org/10.1521/jscp.23.3.413.35460

2. Interview with the author, September 2019

3. Andrea Bonoir, "7 Ways to Build Trust in a Relationship," *Psychology Today*, Sussex Publishers, December 12, 2018, https://www.psychologytoday.com/us/blog/friendship-20/201812/7-ways-build-trust-in-relationship?collection=1134654

Finding Belonging in a Hypermobile World

1. Wei Lu, Alexandre Tanzi, "More People Are Leaving NYC Daily Than Any Other U.S. City," Bloomberg.com, *Bloomberg*, August 29, 2019, https://www.bloomberg.com/news/articles/2019-08-29/new-york-city-metro-area-exodus-soars-to-277-people-every-day

2. Michelle Robertson, "Bay Area Is Top Region for Outward Migration in the U.S.: Here's Where People Are Going," SFGate, *San Francisco Chronicle*, February 9, 2018, https://www.sfgate.com/expensive-san-francisco/article/Bay-Area-outward-migration-exodus-sf-redfin-12563337.php

3. Adam Brinklow, "Survey Says Half of Bay Area Residents Want to Leave California," *Curbed SF,* February 20, 2019, https://sf.curbed.com/2019/2/20/18233498poll-2019-leaving-san-francisco-oakland-silicon-valley

4. Julianne Holt-Lunstad, Timothy B. Smith, J. Bradley Layton. "Social Relationships and Mortality Risk: A Meta-Analytic Review." *PLoS Medicine* 7, no. 7 (2010), https://doi.org/10.1371/journal.pmed.1000316

Be Here Now

1. Eddie (not his real name) in discussion with the author, December 2018.

Make It Work

1. Isaac (not his real name) in discussion with the author, September 2018.

2. Aaron (not his real name) in discussion with the author, December 2017.

#MoNewFriends

1. Nina (not her real name) in discussion with the author, January 2019.

2. Zoya Gervis, "Why the Average American Hasn't Made a New Friend in 5

Years," *New York Post*, May 9, 2019, https://nypost.com/2019/05/09/why-the-average-american-hasnt-made-a-new-friend-in-5-years/

3. Frankie (not her real name) in discussion with the author, January 2018.

4. Bader in discussion with the author, December 2018.

5. Survey by the author, www.adultfriendshipsurvey.com

6. Kate E. Min, Peggy J. Liu, and Soo Kim. "Sharing Extraordinary Experiences Fosters Feelings of Closeness," *Personality and Social Psychology Bulletin* 44, no. 1 (2017): 107–21, https://doi.org/10.1177/0146167217733077

7. Priya Parker, *The Art of Gathering: How We Meet and Why It Matters*, (London, UK: Penguin Business, 2019), Chapter 3: *"Don't Be a Chill Host"*, 71-71.

Get Comfortable

1. Survey by the author, www.adultfriendshipsurvey.com

2. Survey by the author, www.adultfriendshipsurvey.com

3. Transforming Loneliness community conversation with the author, March 2019

Settle In

1. Louis Wirth, "Urbanism as a Way of Life," *American Journal of Sociology 44*, no. 1 (Jul., 1938): 1-24, https://doi.org/10.1086/217913

2. "What Is Walkability?" *Walk Score*, accessed August 2019, https://www.walks-core.com/how-it-works

3. "Cities and Neighborhoods," Walk Score, accessed August 2019, https://www.walkscore.com/cities-and-neighborhoods/

4. Wikipedia contributors, "Walkability," *Wikipedia, The Free Encyclopedia*, https://en.wikipedia.org/w/index.php?title=Walkability&oldid=921057771, accessed August 2019

5. Charles Montgomery, *Happy City: Transforming Our Lives through Urban Design*, 167–70. (Toronto, Ontario: Anchor Canada, 2014). Also: Sarah Goodyear, "Is Traffic Making Us Lonely?," *CityLab*, April 26, 2012, https://www.citylab.com/transportation/2012/04/traffic-making-us-lonely/1858/

6. Wikipedia contributors, "Peak experience," *Wikipedia, The Free Encyclopedia*, https://en.wikipedia.org/w/index.php?title=Peak_experience&oldid=922611065, accessed September 2019

Fitting Friendship into Your Busy Life

1. Generalized Busyness Disorder is not an official term. I made it up. I would define it as a condition in which overstuffed calendars drive us to live in a con-

stant state of rush, stress, FOMO, and the anxious worry that there's never enough time.

2. Sherrie Carter Bourg Psy.D., "Too Busy to Read This? Then You Probably Should: Part II," *Psychology Today*, Sussex Publishers, August 20, 2012, https://www.psychologytoday.com/us/blog/high-octane-women/201208/too-busy-read-then-you-probably-should-part-ii

Get Unbusy
1. (Name withheld) interview with the author, December 2018.
2. Allison Klein, "Want to Be Happier? Stop Scheduling Your Free Time," *The Washington Post*, WP Company, July 31, 2018, https://www.washingtonpost.com/news/inspired-life/wp/2018/07/31/want-to-be-happier-stop-scheduling-your-free-time/

Take Control of Your Time
1. Wikipedia contributors, "Television consumption," *Wikipedia, The Free Encyclopedia*, https://en.wikipedia.org/w/index.php?title=Television_consumption&oldid=918447394, accessed June 2019
2. James Williams, "Why It's OK to Block Ads," Practical Ethics, University of Oxford, October 16, 2015, http://blog.practicalethics.ox.ac.uk/2015/10/why-its-ok-to-block-ads/
Author's note: I read Williams's quote in the book "How to Do Nothing" by Jenny Odell; original source of quote cited above.

Make Room for Spaciousness
1. Jabu in discussion with the author, March 2017.
2. Sophia Gottfried, "Everything About Niksen, The Dutch Concept of Doing Nothing." *Time*, July 12, 2019, https://time.com/5622094/what-is-niksen/

Recontextualize Busy
1. Jed in discussion with the author, April 2019.

Double Down on Showing Up
1. Douglas Nemecek M.D., MBA. ,"Cigna U.S. Loneliness Index," *Cigna*, May 1, 2018, https://www.cigna.com/assets/docs/newsroom/loneliness-survey-2018-full-report.pdf
2. Brené Brown, *Daring Greatly: How the Courage to Be Vulnerable Transforms the Way We*

291

Live, Love, Parent, and Lead, (New York, NY: Avery, An imprint of Penguin Random House, 2012), page 54–54 in Chapter 2: "Debunking the Vulnerability Myths."

3. A nonversation is a blend of non+conversation. It is a meaningless conversation. Wiktionary contributors, "nonversation," *Wiktionary, The Free Dictionary,* https://en.wiktionary.org/w/index.php?title=nonversation&oldid=54359107, accessed October 2019.

4. Lila in discussion with the author, April 2019

Blending Friendship with Partnership and Family

1. Wikipedia contributors, "Dunbar's number," *Wikipedia, The Free Encyclopedia,* https://en.wikipedia.org/w/index.php?title=Dunbar%27s_number&oldid= 918578648, accessed October 2019.

Author's note: One of my favorite visualizations of how Dunbar's "150" correlates to real life comes from Lost Garden, a blog about game design theory, art, and the business of design. There, they visualize Dunbar's Number as Dunbar's Layers showing how smaller clusters make up the 150. Two additional layers are added to account for the fact that we tend to know many more than just 150 people. As Maria Konnikova notes in *The New Yorker,* the size of each cluster tends to be relatively consistent, though people may move between clusters rather fluidly. Dunbar's Layers consist of:

5 Intimate Friends: 200+ hours of bonding time each

10 Best Friends: 200 hours of bonding time each

35 Good Friends: 100 hours of bonding time each

100 Casual Friends: 50 hours of bonding time each

+500 Nodding Acquaintances

+1,500 Recognizable Faces

For additional info, please see:

Daniel Cook, Alexander Youngblood, Amy Jo Kim, Crystin Cox, Erin Hoffman-John, Isaiah Cartwright, Kyle Brink, and Link Hughes, "Social Design Practices for Human-Scale Online Games," *Lost Garden,* December 29, 2018, https://lostgarden.home.blog/2018/12/29/social-design-practices-for-human-scale-online-games/

Maria Konnikova, "The Limits of Friendship," *The New Yorker,* October 7, 2014, https://www.newyorker.com/science/maria-konnikova/social-media-affect-math-dunbar-number-friendships.

2. Ian Sample, "The Price of Love? Losing Two of Your Closest Friends," *The Guardian,* Guardian News and Media, September 15, 2010, https://www.the-

guardian.com/science/2010/sep/15/price-love-close-friends-relationship

Dude, Where's My Friends?

1. Levi (not his real name) in discussion with the author, March 2019.

Lonely Parent

1. Douglas Nemecek M.D., MBA. ,"Cigna U.S. Loneliness Index," *Cigna*, May 1, 2018, https://www.cigna.com/assets/docs/newsroom/loneliness-survey-2018-full-report.pdf

2. Jason McBride, "I Never Expected to Lose so Many Friends after Becoming a Parent," Today's Parent, September 27, 2018, https://www.todaysparent.com/family/parenting/i-never-expected-to-lose-so-many-friends-after-becoming-a-parent/

3. Mia Redrick, "How Women Lose Themselves in Motherhood," *HuffPost*, May 31, 2012, https://www.huffpost.com/entry/motherhood_b_1558981

4. Amy (not her real name) in discussion with the author, May 2019

5. Jordan Rosenfeld, "Motherhood Stole My Identity. Other Women Brought It Back.," *Quartz*, April 3, 2016, https://qz.com/653197/motherhood-stole-my-identity-other-women-brought-it-back/

6. Julie Mitchell, "How New Parents Can Avoid Losing Themselves in Parenthood," *Policygenius Magazine*, March 6, 2017, https://www.policygenius.com/blog/new-parents-can-avoid-losing-parenthood/

7. Rebecca Lang, "The Real Reason It's so Hard to Make Mom Friends," *Motherly*, February 1, 2019, https://www.mother.ly/love/why-is-it-so-hard-to-make-mom-friends

8. Annie in discussion with the author, October 2019.

Parent Town

1. Gabrielle (not her real name) in discussion with the author, August 2019.

2. Richard Florida PhD., "America's Truly Densest Metro Areas," *CityLab*, October 15, 2012, https://www.citylab.com/equity/2012/10/americas-truly-densest-metros/3450/

Keeping Everyone Happy

1. (Name withheld) interview with the author, May 2019.

Outside Looking In

1. Gabrielle (not her real name) in discussion with the author, August 2019.

2. Ruth (not her real name) in discussion with the author, July 2019.

3. Claire Cain Miller and Jonah Engel Bromwich, "How Parents Are Robbing Their Children of Adulthood," *The New York Times,* March 16, 2019, https://www.nytimes.com/2019/03/16/style/snowplow-parenting-scandal.html

4. I learned this activity from Peggy Taylor when I was a facilitator for The Power of Hope. For more activities like this, I highly recommend their trainings and the book *Catch the Fire: An Art-Full Guide to Unleashing the Creative Power of Youth, Adults, and Communities* written by Peggy Taylor and Charlie Murphy, co-founders of PYE: Partners for Youth Empowerment.

Remember to Breathe
1. "Warp and Weft" by Sarah Dunning Park. Poem provided by Park and reprinted with her permission. July 2019

Getting Better at Getting Closer
1. Denise (not her real name) in discussion with the author, 2012.

2. Madison Means, "How Instagram Makes Us Feel Closer To Celebrities," *The Odyssey Online,* April 11, 2016, https://www.theodysseyonline.com/became-friends-with-celebrity-over-social-media

3. Wikipedia contributors, "Parasocial interaction," *Wikipedia, The Free Encyclopedia,* https://en.wikipedia.org/w/index.php?title=Parasocial_interaction&oldid=923838050, accessed August 2019.

4. Sherry Turkle, *Alone Together: Why We Expect More from Technology and Less from Each Other.* (New York, NY: Basic Books, 2017)

5. (Name withheld) interview with the author, November 2018.

6. Angelica (not her real name) in discussion with the author, December 2018.

7. Julia in discussion with the author, December 2018.

Imaginary Friends
1. Gavin Whitner, "Podcast Statistics (2019) – Newest Available Data + Infographic," *Music Oomph,* November 5, 2019, https://musicoomph.com/podcast-statistics/

2. Jaclyn Peiser, "Podcast Growth Is Popping in the U.S., Survey Shows," *The New York Times,* March 6, 2019. https://www.nytimes.com/2019/03/06/business/media/podcast-growth.html

3. Steven Simonitch, "Japan's First 'Cuddle Cafe' Lets You Sleep with a Stranger for Y6,000 an Hour," *Japan Today,* October 3, 2012,

https://japantoday.com/category/features/lifestyle/japans-first-cuddle-cafe-lets-you-sleep-with-a-stranger-for-y6000-an-hour ;

Roc Morin, "The Booming Japanese Rent-a-Friend Business," *The Atlantic,* Atlantic Media Company, November 7, 2017, https://www.theatlantic.com/family/archive/2017/11/paying-for-fake-friends-and-family/545060/

4. Douglas Nemecek M.D., MBA. ,"Cigna U.S. Loneliness Index," *Cigna*, May 1, 2018, https://www.cigna.com/assets/docs/newsroom/loneliness-survey-2018-full-report.pdf

Ask Better Questions

1. Alison Wood Brooks and Leslie K. John, "The Surprising Power of Questions," *Harvard Business Review*, May 2018. https://hbr.org/2018/05/the-surprising-power-of-questions

So Awkward

1. (Name withheld) in discussion with the author, June 2019.

2. Jack in discussion with the author, January 2019.

3. Wikipedia contributors, "Emotion," *Wikipedia, The Free Encyclopedia*, https://en.wikipedia.org/w/index.php?title=Emotion&oldid=920388947, accessed October 2019.

Author's note: Paul Ekman originally named 6 universally-recognized (regardless of culture) emotions. Later, Robert Plutchik expanded the list of emotions to 8. More recently, Dacher Keltner and Daniel Cordaro (former students of Ekman) completed research that expanded the list of universally-experienced emotions to 27.

4. Marilyn Wei, "There Are 27 Different Emotions, New Study Suggests," *Psychology Today*, Sussex Publishers, September 11, 2017, https://www.psychology-today.com/us/blog/urban-survival/201709/there-are-27-different-emotions-new-study-suggests

5. Taylor (not her real name) in discussion with the author, January 2019.

6. Melissa Dahl, "Why Trying to Be Less Awkward Never Works." *The New York Times*, February 13, 2018, https://www.nytimes.com/2018/02/13/smarter-living/dont-be-less-awkward.html

7. Jack in discussion with the author, January 2019.

8. Author's note: I wasn't able to find the exact creator of this technique, as the "5-4-3-2-1 technique/method" produces numerous sources online and it appears to be a tool that therapists have been using for many years, so I would like to give

credit to Young Women Empowered; I was co-leading a weekend retreat camp for them in July 2019 and one of the youth leaders taught this exercise to the group during as a grounding and centering tool. For more information about YWE's programs, please visit y-we.org

Face the Music

1. Jack in discussion with the author, January 2019.
2. Ella (not her real name) in discussion with the author, January 2019.
3. Wikiquote contributors, "Len Wein," *Wikiquote*, Wikimedia Foundation, Inc., May 13, 2019, https://en.wikiquote.org/wiki/Len_Wein, accessed September 2019
4. Jamie Utt, "Intent vs. Impact: Why Your Intentions Don't Really Matter," *Everyday Feminism*, July 30, 2013, https://everydayfeminism.com/2013/07/intentions-dont-really-matter/

Ask for Help

1. Olivia (not her real name) in discussion with the author, January 2019.
2. Participant at"Cultivating the Garden of Friendship" workshop, April 2019
3. Julia in discussion with the author, December 2018.
4. Beth in discussion with the author, December 2018.
5. Linda (not her real name) in discussion with the author, July 2019.
6. Marian (not real name) in discussion with the author, April 2019.
7. Wikipedia contributors, "Social support: Categories and definitions," *Wikipedia, The Free Encyclopedia*, https://en.wikipedia.org/w/index.php?title=Social_support&oldid=924752903, accessed October 2019
8. Wikipedia contributors, "Social support: Benefits," Wikipedia, The Free Encyclopedia, https://en.wikipedia.org/w/index.php?title=Social_support&oldid=924752903
9. Michelle Debczak, "Change Your Smoke Detector Batteries With Your Clocks This Weekend," *Mental Floss*, March 9, 2016, https://www.mentalfloss.com/article/76842/change-your-smoke-detector-batteries-your-clocks-weekend

From Friendship to Community

1. Jeannie in discussion with the author, December 2018.
2. Tim Henderson, "More Americans Living Alone, Census Says," *The Washington Post*, WP Company, September 28, 2014, https://www.washingtonpost.com/politics/more-americans-living-alone-census-says/2014/09/28/67e1d02e-473a-11e4-b72e-d60a9229cc10_story.html

296 WE SHOULD GET TOGETHER

Making It Real

1. Randall (not his real name) in discussion with the author, March 2017.

2. Richard L. Florida PhD., *Who's Your City? How the Creative Economy Is Making Where to Live the Most Important Decision of Your Life* (New York, NY: Basic Books, 2008), Chapter 11: *"Cities Have Personalities, Too,"* 190-213.

3. Nastaran Tavakoli-Far, "The Why Factor - Female Friendships - BBC Sounds," *BBC News*, BBC, July 30, 2018, https://www.bbc.co.uk/sounds/play/w3cswrk8

4. Brian Joseph Gillespie, Janet Lever, David Frederick, and Tracy Royce, "Close Adult Friendships, Gender, and the Life Cycle," *Journal of Social and Personal Relationships* 32, no. 6 (August 26, 2014): 709–36, https://doi.org/10.1177/0265407514546977

5. Douglas Nemecek M.D., MBA. ,"Cigna U.S. Loneliness Index," *Cigna*, May 1, 2018, https://www.cigna.com/assets/docs/newsroom/loneliness-survey-2018-full-report.pdf

Kat Vellos is an experience designer, facilitator, and the founder of *Better Than Small Talk* and *Bay Area Black Designers* which was profiled in Forbes. Kat has a passion for cultivating community and designing experiences that help others connect more authentically. She offers *We Should Get Together* to help more adults create fulfilling friendships that last a lifetime. She lives in Berkeley CA and loves tacos.

weshouldgettogether.com
katvellos.com

If you enjoyed this book, please consider writing a review online to help other people discover it.

Photographs of the author by Jamie Nease

CPSIA information can be obtained
at www.ICGtesting.com
Printed in the USA
LVHW080953031020
667414LV00036B/16